Acquisitions, Budgets and Material Costs: Issues and Approaches

About the Editor

Sul H. Lee, Dean of the University Libraries, University of Oklahoma, is an internationally recognized leader and consultant in the library administration and management field. Mr. Lee is a member of the Board of Governors of the Research Libraries Group as well as a member of the Committee on the Management of Research Libraries, Association of Research Libraries. His works include *Pricing and Costs of Monographs and Serials: National and International Issues*. He is the editor of the *Journal of Library Administration*.

Acquisitions, Budgets and Material Costs: Issues and Approaches

Sul H. Lee
Editor

The Haworth Press
New York • London

Acquisitions, Budgets and Material Costs: Issues and Approaches is monographic supplement #2 to *Journal of Library Administration*. It is not supplied as part of the subscription to the journal, but is available from the publisher at an additional charge.

The Haworth Press, Inc., 12 West 32 Street, New York, NY 10001
EUROSPAN/Haworth, 3 Henrietta Street, London WC2E 8LU England

Library of Congress Cataloging-in-Publication Data

Acquisitions, budgets and material costs.

    (Monographic supplement #2 to Journal of library administration)
    Bibliography: p.
    Includes index.
    1. Acquisitions (Libraries). 2. Library finance. 3. Library materials – Prices. 4. Approval plans in library acquisitions. I. Lee, Sul H. II. Series: Monographic supplement ... to Journal of library administration ; #2.
Z689.A274   1987   025.2'1   87-29867
ISBN 0-86656-690-2

For Melissa

CONTENTS

Introduction

On February 26 and 27, 1987 a national conference focusing on acquisitions processes, material costs and library budgeting convened under the sponsorship of the University of Oklahoma Libraries and the University of Oklahoma Foundation. Conference registrants from 24 states and 2 Canadian provinces came together to hear and discuss papers presented by librarians and vendor representatives.

Demands on librarians to find better budget management strategies and to develop more effective material acquisition processes have created an environment in which librarians and book vendors are examining their methods of acquiring and supplying materials to libraries. There is very real pressure on libraries to justify expenditures and methods by which collections are developed. These conference papers present some of the recent studies and ideas about acquisition processes and the management of material costs.

In "The Importance of Approval Plans When Budgets are Lean," Tom Leonhardt, Dean, University Libraries, University of the Pacific, discusses the significant role approval plans can play when resources do not keep pace with costs. Karen Schmidt, Head, Acquisitions, University of Illinois, reviews the current role and the handling of approval plans in academic libraries and suggests a new approach for the publisher-based plan.

Jean L. Loup, Head of the Documents Center and Senior Associate Librarian, University of Michigan, discusses a study of approval plans in 28 ARL Libraries. This Council on Library Resources funded study analyzes the approval plans to determine if the collecting patterns were similar. Ms. Loup presents the findings in "Analysis of Approval Plans in ARL Libraries."

The impact of inflation is examined by Dana Alessi, Division Sales Manager, Blackwell North America. In her presentation, "Up the Elevator: An Examination of Approval Plan Inflation and its Impact on Libraries," she reviews the increasing costs of titles in selected subject disciplines, discusses causes for the costs, and assesses the ramifications for libraries and suppliers. Edna Laughrey, Head, Acquisitions, University of Michigan, describes the results of other studies examining the effect of inflation and devaluation of the U.S. dollar in "Projecting Material Costs: Basis for Effective Decision Making."

Fred Lynden, Assistant University Librarian for Technical Services, Brown University, develops the process of materials budgeting from the collection of data to the justification of the budget in "Managing Rising Materials Costs." Special attention is given to discriminatory pricing and methods for counteracting the weakening of the dollar.

With the development of new technology and the dissemination of information using new technologies, the library materials budget has felt the impact of new information formats. Jennifer Cargill, Associate Director of Libraries for Information Access and Systems, Texas Tech University, examines this issue in "CD-ROM Databases, and Other New Information Formats: Their Acquisition." Lenore Clark, Coordinator of Collection Development, University of Oklahoma completes the volume with "Acquisitions, Budgets and Materials Costs: A Selected Bibliography."

The conference contained many opportunities for questions and discussion among the speakers and participants. Unfortunately, it is not possible to report the many comments and views expressed during these exchanges. We are, however, pleased to present the edited conference papers in this volume and hope the information and insights are valuable to the reader.

I want to express my gratitude to Wilbur Stolt, Director of Library Public Services, University of Oklahoma, Rodney Hersberger, Director, California State College Library, Bakersfield, and Coy Harmon, Dean of Libraries, Murray State University, for their excellent editorial assistance. Don Hudson provided outstanding administrative support to the conference and Pat Webb was instrumental in the preparation of this publication.

Sul H. Lee

The Importance of Approval Plans
When Budgets Are Lean

Thomas W. Leonhardt

How many times have you heard colleagues say that approval plans are great if you are rich but their budgets barely provide enough to meet the essential demands. Perhaps you have made the same point yourself: I can not afford an approval plan.

Which one can you not afford? Approval plans come in all shapes and sizes and range in costs from the foreign plans that cost the Library of Congress more than $1.5 million a year to smaller plans for art exhibition catalogs, for example, that cost about $2,000 a year.

Before going any further I should define an approval plan as "dealer selection orders," as the University of Toronto calls them, with return for credit privileges. I do not limit approval plans to those comprehensive programs that are designed to cover the full LC or Dewey classes and all publishers. Early approval and gathering plan conferences were pretty much devoted to comprehensive plans. Cost was a big concern because some of those plans were expensive. That is probably when librarians first began to think they could not afford approval plans. We thought too big and too narrowly. I do, however, include the comprehensive plans in my definition and even believe that they can be adapted for libraries with lean budgets.

By the end of this paper I hope that you will catch yourself about to say you cannot afford an approval plan. Instead, you will consider what it is you need within your budget and design your approval plan accordingly.

I maintain that once you decide what materials you ought to acquire above all others, you can afford an approval plan. I maintain that if you have the most modest of budgets and are in an academic library, you can afford an approval plan. I maintain that if you are in budget difficulties because of cuts or insufficient increases, and you know

Thomas W. Leonhardt is Dean, University Libraries at the University of the Pacific.

what you need to support faculty programs, you cannot afford not to have an approval plan.

What I want to demonstrate today is that approval plans are not only for the rich but also for those libraries with small budgets or with budgets that have been cut. Approval plans offer opportunities to make the most of each acquisitions dollar spent, keep development of the collection even, and take advantage of efficiencies and economies available through book-in-hand processing.

I also want to demonstrate that many of the arguments for and against approval plans are really expressions of attitudes. I happen to think that approval plans, approached correctly, offer many advantages over regular, so-called firm orders. If you suspect that I have less tolerance for arguments against approval plans than those for approval plans, you are correct and ought to keep that in mind as you hear what I have to say.

As I prepared these remarks I was tempted to summarize the history of approval plans but that has already been done and, besides, I think such a summary would confuse the issues I want to talk about. I really want to discuss the approval plans of today, not of yesterday.

The approval plans of today developed in the 1970s but librarians today seem to be more aware of them and booksellers are promoting them more aggressively as a way of competing in a tight market. You decide what it is you want and there will be at least one bookseller (probably five or six) who will sit down with you and help design an approval plan to your satisfaction.

Despite all of the attention and discussion devoted to approval plans over the years, librarians do not always agree on what an approval plan is or is not. As I mentioned earlier, a bookseller will agree with your own definition, if you can explain it adequately, because he wants to sell you books. This confusion or ambiguity stems from the protean character of approval plans. Approval plans are all things to all people and as such can be powerful collection development tools and they can help streamline processing and cataloging, but they can also get a library into trouble, if not handled well.

It is also easy to argue for and against approval plans because of their ambiguities. You can twist them into any shape you like and can play to the needs and fears of those who know little about approval plans or who are predisposed toward or against them. If your faculty believe that an approval plan is an abdication of selection responsibilities, you can play to their beliefs. If they believe that their budget is being stolen, you can play to their beliefs. If they believe those things and you do not, you can probably convince them that an approval plan has merit and will help them. And if you cannot convince them you are right, you can probably get them to give you a chance.

APPROVAL PLAN LITERATURE

Although I am not going to summarize the history of approval plans I would like to say a few words about the literature of approval plans. This is an important and growing body of literature that has helped legitimize approval plans for thousands of librarians.

Since 1969 there have been four international conferences devoted to approval plans and in 1984, this Oklahoma City Conference featured five (out of seven) papers on approval plans.[1] There have been numerous other speeches and articles about approval plans since Richard Abel introduced his variation on blanket plans of the post-World War II era.

By 1972, Kathleen McCullough was able to cite twenty-nine articles dealing, at least in part, with approval plans or methods of acquiring publications automatically.[2] In her survey, McCullough raised the question of in-breeding within the approval plan literature: "Libraries with approval plans of their own will not find much in this list that is outside their experience. Almost every author has been cited by another; there is much in-breeding, a situation suggesting the need for more research.[3]

If McCullough compiled a similar list today it would be much longer but she could still make the comments about experience and in-breeding. It is true, in reading the literature on approval plans, one can usually relate to much of what has been written but I am certain that almost fifteen years later, the literature contains much of value for all librarians using or contemplating approval plans. It is a rich literature that is worth reading and, from time-to-time, re-reading. One of the benefits of sharing our thoughts, experiments, and experiences with each other is that we are often able to gain a better grasp of what we are doing or attempting to do by having someone else verbalize a concept. This is why we attend acquisitions conferences, management skills workshops, and other forms of continuing education. If we are really lucky, we will learn something new, but we can not lose if we are simply reminded of things we had learned once and forgotten.

Is there still in-breeding to be found in the literature on approval plans? Yes, but that is not necessarily bad and it really ought to be expected when you consider the limited number of practitioners and researchers who are likely to be writing on the subject. A possible danger in citing each other continually is that our articles will all start to look and sound alike and we will lose our vitality. If we are going to cite each other (we can not cite what is not there) we must be alert to the need to read and listen to each other critically and build on what has gone before. We must not be afraid to disagree with one another, not on a personal level but constructively and responsibly.

McCullough, Axford, and several others have called for more research on approval plans. In general, yes, we must recognize the need for objective studies, research, if you will, but as practitioners, we often have to deliver thoughtful essays that may refer to research but that are usually based on experience and the thoughtful essays of others. There is an inherent danger in too much reliance on essays to the exclusion of research and studies.

We must also conduct and report on independent original studies and that is really what McCullough was getting at. When we begin to cite secondary sources, no matter how well-respected the author is, we begin to build a credo based on opinion, belief, and faith. We end up with a religion rather than a body of knowledge.

One thing to keep in mind about these studies is that they often rely on opinion. Opinions can be important but opinions are not necessarily facts and indisputable. They are clues and we need to use them as such.

Surveys are also important for their revelation of patterns. We do not want to do something just because everyone else is doing it. I do not think we want to reject something out of hand, either, just because they are popular or widespread. There is a certain wisdom in trying something that others, leaders in their fields, have tried and found useful.

USE OF APPROVAL PLANS

The use of approval plans is widespread. Shirk and Reidelbach surveyed eight major domestic approval plan vendors and found that they administered 1,099 approval plans including 296 comprehensive plans.[4] There may be some duplication of libraries, that is, the 1,099 plans may not correlate with 1,099 different libraries but there are still going to be several hundred libraries that use such plans.

In 1969, Norman Dudley surveyed the Association of Research Libraries and found that 85% of ARL libraries had at least one approval plan, either foreign or domestic.[5] In 1975, McCullough et al. surveyed 101 academic libraries and determined that 79.2% had an approval plan.[6] In 1981 I surveyed the Association of Research Libraries and found that 85% of the membership had at least one approval plan.[7]

When Clint Howard finishes his upcoming survey, preliminary to updating the SPEC Kit on Approval Plans, he will find at least 85% of ARL libraries use approval plans.

I wonder, however, if the number of vendors offering approval plans will have increased. In 1981, there were over 200 approval vendors named by the ARL respondents, including 53 publishers. Vendors named in the survey specialized in providing materials from geographical areas or by format such as audio visual, sound recordings, music scores, art exhibition catalogs, Belles Lettres, small presses, university presses, and general scholarly works.[8]

The reason I wonder is that I really do not have any idea. Many booksellers provide approval plans but some have resisted and have concentrated on standing orders and firm orders. Lest I be misunderstood and lead you astray, I do not advocate approval plans to the exclusion of other methods of acquisition. There is a strong market for booksellers who can respond to firm orders quickly and responsibly. As much as I tout approval plans, I do not consider them panaceas or replacements for other methods of acquisition. An approval plan is just another tool and even libraries with comprehensive plans need the bookseller who can provide those materials outside the approval plan profile.

What do these statistics mean? They show that most of the large research libraries and many of the medium-size and small academic libraries of the U.S. use approval plans. Some use a half a dozen or more. The implication is that they consider approval plans a credible way to buy library materials. Approval plans are used to acquire all kinds of library materials from all over the world with all levels of budgets. And approval plans are justified for all kinds of reasons.

PROCESSING ECONOMIES

Approval plans are usually thought of as collection development tools but they also relate directly to the acquisitions process and, by extension, to the cataloging process. I would like to include this aspect of approval plans in my discussion. A lean book budget hints that there may also be a lean personnel budget. New programs needing additional staff may have to begin, if they begin at all, using current staff and with inadequate resources.

William Axford, in 1971, elaborately argued that approval plans saved processing costs and could reduce the cost of acquiring a book by as much as six clerical positions depending on internal procedures.[9] In the ARL survey I conducted in 1980/81,[10] Michigan State University reported that it saved several hours a week by using an approval plan rather than regular ordering but that the savings did not add up to a position. I would not argue for an approval plan solely on the basis of projected staff savings but I think that an approval plan, because of its book-in-hand nature, must lead to some processing efficiencies and this ought to be taken into account when considering the use of an approval plan. The potential for processing efficiencies is greater now than ever before.

In 1969, Dick Boss, then at the University of Utah, reported that his library had automated (key punched) its acquisitions except for approval receipts. Those did not fit into the automated scheme and had to be accounted for manually, an extra step. The system did not save time or staff.[11]

All these reports were before the widespread use of microcomputer acquisitions systems, some of which interface with national bibliographic databases. I have not collected and analyzed cost statistics the way Axford did, but assuming that his study is essentially correct, the potential for savings today is much greater than in 1969 or even in 1981 when Michigan State reported its savings. And the systems that handle firm orders efficiently have an equally efficient capacity for approval plans, unlike the early systems like the one Dick Boss described.

When Axford studied acquisitions procedures, including pre-order searching, MARC and OCLC were in their infancy and there was no CIP or ISBN. There were no microcomputers as we know and use them, and no true online acquisitions systems that did not involve key-punching and manual filing. There was no RLIN (BALLOTS was still being developed), UTLAS (as now constituted), or WLN.

Today, the elimination of a firm order means the elimination of at least one step and possibly more depending on a library, its utilities, and how it takes advantage of them.

Even if a library has no automated system, book-in-hand (non-purchase order) acquisition should still be faster, more efficient, and more accurate than ordering books title by title. And the library's clientele should be better served because the books will reach the library faster by several weeks even if a firm order is placed soon after publication. In practice, the book may not be ordered for several weeks or months after publication because the selector did not find out about the publication until then or did not have time to submit an order until then. If the selector is the only person who is going to want to use that book (many selectors believe that to be the case) there is no harm done, but when others read a review, the hope is that the title will already be available in the Library.

Most libraries in the U.S. belong to UTLAS, WLN, RLIN, or OCLC. With book in hand, the acquisitions search can also be the cataloging search. If series and serials have been eliminated from approval plans (they should be to simplify matters and give better accounting for those kinds of publications), the book in hand can be cataloged without bothering to file an on-order/in-process slip in the public catalog. Instead, the book is cataloged, without even a workshop being printed and quickly made available to the library's users. This immediate cataloging saves work for the Acquisitions Department and probably for the Catalog Department, too. It will mean revising the technical processing work flow but should be worth the effort.

For those libraries with automated systems that interface with a bibliographic utility, the cataloging and acquisitions (fund accounting, vendor statistics, etc.) steps are virtually combined into one. This is especially true of libraries using OCLC's CATME (Cataloging MicroEnhancer) software where search results, including all bibliographic data, initiated in acquisitions, can be stored on diskettes and forwarded with the books to the catalog department. Some libraries are already doing this and I urge them to report on their experiences, good and bad.

Librarians who doubt that this will work should perform some internal comparisons. Whether the hypothesis is true or not, these internal studies ought to be shared with other institutions. We owe it to ourselves to find more efficient ways to operate. We cannot be satisfied with getting by the same old way.

Remember, too, that much pre-order searching has to be repeated when a book finally arrives, especially if no LC copy was found during that search. Book-in-hand processing through approval plans (or gifts, exchanges, etc.) eliminates the double search most of the time, with the actual percentage depending on the hit rate for acceptable cataloging copy.

BUDGET

There seem to be two major budget issues related to approval plans: affordability and flexibility. SPEC Kit # 83[12] includes documents that argue from both sides of the fence. Both issues, affordability and flexibility, are really non-issues and the arguments for and against approval plans really say more about one's attitudes about budgets, approval plans, and collection development than about the pros and cons of approval plans. That sounds simplistic but attitudes can and do have profound effects on the success of programs and projects.

For example, if one's attitude towards the budget is proprietary, one is reluctant to commit it in advance of anything other than a regular order. Encumbering $25 to $50 at a time seems all that such a mindset can handle comfortably. If the library's collection development program is really committed to acquiring what it can afford of its fair share of current publishing output, does it really matter whether the books come automatically, via approval, or one by one, via regular ordering? It does, but for reasons other than the budget.

If there are $100,000 worth of university press books that you feel your library ought to acquire, you ought to be setting that money aside, one way or another. One of the reasons many academic libraries have university press approval plans is because they found, over the years, that they were buying most of them anyway. Planning the budget to accommodate these collection development needs through an approval plan is not losing flexibility, it is budgeting soundly and providing flexibility. The money that is left is free to be spent, flexibly, on regular orders and out of print materials. Once a library knows how much money is needed to support its approval plan, prepayments and negotiated discount can actually provide increased flexibility for other needs by earning hundreds or thousands of dollars.

Affordability of approval plans is really a state of mind. To say that we can not afford an approval plan makes as much sense as saying we can not afford a standing order or a subscription and then buying the series title by title or a journal, issue by issue off the newsstand.

It is true that the budget allocation for approval plans is not as flexible as with regular firm orders, just as the serials allocation is not as flexible. With firm orders, when the money runs out, the ordering stops. Based on the previous year's expenditures, including new titles added, and an estimate about inflation, price increases, postage hikes, and foreign exchange rates, a careful, educated guess must be made each year about what the serials bill is going to be.

The same kind of inflexibility exists with approval plans, especially if you are going to establish a deposit account (prepayment). A deposit account should bring extra discounts or it should be earning interest so that you can buy some flexibility with that approach. But is flexibility really the issue here, any more than it is for the serials budget? If we were committing our non-library materials budget to fixed items (supplies, equipment, personnel) at the very beginning of the fiscal year and were allowed no variations between what we could spend in each category and even what we could spend on given items, that would be an inflexible budget. We do not always know what our needs are going to be six months from now. We may decide that spending money on a student project is more important than buying an ergonomic computer table. We need the flexibility to make those decisions.

An approval plan that has been carefully thought out and that is guided by a profile reflecting current needs is not in the same category as equipment, personnel, and supplies. There should be money set aside for the items that fall outside our profile but we do not build collections title by title. We do not say, well, this looks good, it fits Prof. Brown's research interests, and it will support a class that is taught each semester but it is only November and there may be an even better title coming out in the spring. If there is, you probably ought to have both. And the one in the spring may not come out or it may not be as good or better than the book you already know about. Do you tell Prof. Brown that the reason the book is not in the library is that you were waiting for a better one to come along, perhaps at a bargain price? Now Prof. Brown wants you to order it and you are weeks or months behind other libraries and your patron has to wait. If he is a reasonable person he will not bear a grudge against you but he will remember the incident when it recurs or when he finally gets the book, after his class is over or his paper has been submitted.

For monographs, libraries generally do not distinguish between current imprints and back list titles. There is some distinction between in-print and out-of-print but even then, there must be very few libraries that assign a fixed dollar amount to out-of-print ordering from antiquarian catalogs and even fewer who distinguish between current imprints (say current and previous imprint years) and imprints three or more years old.

When we say we can not afford an approval plan, are we not really admitting that we do not know what we want? Or, we don't want to spend the time developing a profile or, we honestly do not think an approval plan meets our needs and is not a good way to go. That is fine, but let us not deceive ourselves about affordability.

COLLECTION DEVELOPMENT

Early approval plans were sometimes referred to as gathering plans and blanket plans, thus acknowledging the precursors of the approval plan as developed by Richard Abel in the early 1960s. (For a concise history of approval plans see Vosper, 1980.)[13] Perhaps we have gone too far in our emphasis on the approval part of the plans and should return to the concept of gathering. The return privilege may be important (in some cases, however, it is cheaper to give the book away) but the real purpose of an approval plan is to build a useful library collection in a way that meets the needs of the present and the future.

To really feel comfortable with an approval plan and use it as an automatic gathering of useful material (not necessarily material that will circulate heavily immediately upon receipt), librarians and faculty (I am speaking primarily of academic libraries), need to disavow themselves of the notion that anyone, anywhere, at any time has really and truly known exactly what should and should not be acquired by a library. It is an impossible task for several reasons.

First of all, it is impossible for any one person, library staff, book seller, agent, or whatever to know all that is being published. Even if that were possible, it would be even more difficult to know which publications are going to become the standard works that will endure beyond our lifetimes. Even if we could read all those books before deciding on what to purchase, we cannot know what the future programs and research interests will be in our institutions five or ten years from now. Would you necessarily recognize a seminal work if you read one? In how many fields? Are you willing to wait for future readers in other places to identify such works before you try to acquire them? Will you wait for a reviewer to venture an opinion about the worth of a book before you order it? In certain areas, does it even matter if the reviewer pans the book? There are certain works by certain authors or publishers that the library must acquire regardless of critical acceptance. And will the right reviewer review the right book? If not, then waiting for a review will not likely lead to the acquisition of the right book in a timely fashion. It is little consolation to wait until someone else selects the work for you only to find that more methodical and sure-handed collectors have caused it to go out of print.

The only way you can guarantee that you are getting every title you need is to buy every title that is published. There are libraries with resources that allow them to acquire comprehensively in certain areas but no library in the world has the money or the space to collect everything that is published. Choices have to be made.

Books may be ordered title by title, but rarely do we consider them on their intellectual and scholarly merits title by title. Some books are reviewed, but we cannot wait for reviews. We have to anticipate demand. We have to order on blind faith, faith in the publisher, for the most part, faith in an author only when we recognize the author's name.

It is not uncommon, especially toward the end of the fiscal year, for academic departments to send to the acquisitions department, publishers' catalogs marked "Order all we don't have." The catalogs tend to be from well-known, accepted, reputable publishers of scholarly and professional books. Chances are, most of those items are already in the library, on order, or expected on approval or standing order.

What this means is that librarians, booksellers, and faculty members recognize, at varying levels, that publishers have selected what we need and we, in turn, select what we can afford of those materials fitting our programs. The publisher, in business to make money, hires acquisitions editors to go in the field and find out what is needed and then find someone who is willing and capable of producing a publishable work. That is where book selection really begins.

I am not saying that everything being published is of high quality and deserving to see the light of day. Some might argue quite convincingly that with the growth of knowledge and the need to publish or perish, a lot of marginal material is being published. But publishers survive and build reputations on consistent quality. I am not cynical enough to assume that more than a small percentage of the books being published are a waste of time and paper. Most of what is published is reasonably good and is published because there is a demand for it.

Some publishers are better than others but even so, libraries will seldom want everything by the better publishers and should not ignore the output of the more questionable publishers.

When we establish an approval plan, we work with a vendor to determine which of those pre-selected (by the publisher) titles we will get to examine before purchasing.

When the books arrive, we can see if the established names are living up to their reputations and we can see if the publications of the questionable publishers have merit. In a sense, we are now selecting at the title-by-title level but in fact we are only looking for signs of quality such as bibliographies, notes, indexes, illustrations, and so on. Scanning the books gives us only a general idea of their true value. We cannot afford the time to read them and even if we did, we would not in good conscience, be able to reject very many of them.

Do you still hesitate because you fear that, through an approval plan, you will be building a collection identical to hundreds of others, especially on a small budget? You probably are anyway to the extent that we all read the same reviews and rely on the reputations of authors and publishers in all fields. Face it, there is always going to be a certain amount of duplication among our collections because there is a core of material that we all need. Does it really matter how we acquire it? Do we express as much concern for duplication through firm orders, gifts, and exchanges as we do for approval plans? Is it really an issue or an excuse? Once we know what we want, that is, the core material, do we not have an obligation to acquire it as quickly, efficiently, and economically as possible?

CONCLUSION

What does all this have to do with poor libraries, libraries with lean budgets? Before approval plans can be sold to the constituents of a library, poor or otherwise, a case has to be made for approval plans as a sound library practice, a practice that will benefit the library in the way that it acquires and processes materials and the way such acquisitions support the needs of the library's constituency.

Once we make the case for approval plans in general, we need to ask how one might be used by a library with a lean budget. In general terms, that should be obvious by now, but there are ways in which we can apply approval plan generalities to our own specific needs and purposes.

Even if we cannot afford a rich, comprehensive plan, we can (and should) build on our strengths and work to overcome weaknesses; collecting strengths and support weaknesses (lack of subject specialists, for example). We need to identify the strengths of our collections. If American literature and U.S. history are strong programs, base your approval plan on those subject areas.

If the library does not have a written collection development policy, developing an approval plan profile, even on known strengths, can be a first step in writing such a policy. Sometimes we have to begin by stating the obvious. And if there is a written policy, developing an approval plan profile can lead to revisions in the policy.[14]

Now we can really talk about affordability. Libraries with lean budgets cannot afford not to invest what they have into programs designed to automatically bring in those materials that they must have. The investment could be in American literature, U.S. history, art exhibition catalogs, music scores, talking books, and so on. The list goes on and on.

In dollars and cents, my ARL survey found that the median approval plan expenditure as a percent of the library materials budget was 8.9, the mean was 9.7.[15] That leaves over 90% of the budget for other things, including other or expanded approval plans. The key is knowing what you really ought to be collecting as a first priority, knowing how much you have to spend on these essential materials, and then determining how you are going to acquire that material as quickly, as efficiently, and as economically as possible. For materials just coming into print, a custom made approval plan is your best bet.

NOTES

1. Sul H. Lee, ed., *Issues in Acquisitions: Programs & Evaluations*, (Ann Arbor, Mich.: Pierian Press, 1984).

2. Kathleen McCullough, "Approval Plans: Vendor Responsibility and Library Research. A Literature Survey and Discussion," *College and Research Libraries* 33(September 1972):368-381.

3. Ibid., 368.

4. John H. Reidelbach and Gary M. Shirk, "Selecting An Approval Plan Vendor II: Comparative Vendor Data," *Library Acquisitions: Practice and Theory*, 8(1984):169-171.

5. Norman Dudley, "The Blanket Order," *Library Trends*, 18(January 1980): 318-327.

6. Kathleen McCullough, Edwin D. Posey, and Doyle C. Pickett, *Approval Plans and Academic Libraries: An Interpretive Survey*, (Phoenix, Ariz.: Oryx Press, 1977), 9.

7. Thomas W. Leonhardt, ed., *Approval Plans in ARL Libraries*, Association of Research Office of Management Studies Systems and Procedures Exchange Center SPEC Flyer/Kit 83 (Washington, D.C., 1982).

8. Ibid. 11-15.

9. H. William Axford, "Economics of Approval Plans," in *Economics of Approval Plans*, Peter Spyers-Duran and Daniel Gore, ed., (Westport, Ct.: Greenwood Press, 1972), 3-23.

10. Leonhardt, *Approval Plans*, 59-60.

11. Richard W. Boss, "Automation and Approval Plans," in *Advances in Understanding Approval and Gathering Plans in Academic Libraries*, ed. Peter Spyers-Duran and Daniel Gore (Kalamazoo: Western Michigan University, 1970), 19-29.

12. Leonhardt, *Approval Plans*, 4-5.

13. Robert Vosper, "The Blanket Order: Some Historical Footnotes and Conjectures," in *Shaping Library Collections for the 1980s*, ed. Peter Spyers-Duran and Thomas Mann, Jr. (Phoenix, Ariz.: Oryx Press, 1980), 4-17.

14. Noreen S. Alldredge, "The Symbiotic Relationship of Approval Plans and Collection Development," in *Shaping Library Collections for the 1980s*, 174-177.

15. Leonhardt, *Approval Plans*, 2.

Firstest with the Mostest:
Publisher-Based Approval Plans
in Academic Libraries

Karen A. Schmidt

Stonewall Jackson was a successful military strategist, known for his determination and intelligence in battle. One of his secrets for success on the battlefield was his method of concentrating forces, sending in his men to be "the firstest with the mostest."[1] He may not have won the war, but he did win the battle, using this approach. When I was young, we used this phrase to indicate the very best. It meant that one had brought together the most resources and got there first, winning out over the others. I believe that approval plans can provide the same strategy for collecting in academic libraries, if they are developed carefully and interpreted in the context of the individual library.

This paper examines and redefines some of the issues of approval plans and explores the positive impact of a reworking of the publisher-based plan for academic libraries. It is important to point out that approval plans are different from gathering plans. Approval plans are those in which selection and rejection of books are decided continuously by librarians. There is constant intervention by the vendor and the librarian in the procurement of books. Gathering plans, as in the case of blanket orders, do not involve returns or constant intervention by the librarian or vendor. This distinction is essential to any discussion of approval plans and will be described in greater detail later.

Practically everything that can be said about the usefulness of approval plans has been said. Approval plans are found in almost all academic libraries, in one form or another. Our profession generally agrees that approval plans are an efficient way to procure books, both in terms of staff economy and price discounts. What has not been explored deeply enough is how these various plans can affect the orga-

Karen A. Schmidt is Head of Acquisitions at the University of Illinois-Urbana.

nization of our libraries, the level of professional work, and both staff and materials budgets.

Approval plans come in many shapes and sizes. Probably the most common configuration is a subject-based plan which encompasses any number of subjects. In this situation, a library prescribes to a vendor the subjects in which materials are to be collected and the level at which each subject should be treated. When this "profile" (a coded description of the subject and their levels) is established, and the terms of discount and handling are arranged, the library begins to receive books on a regular basis. The vendor takes upon itself the responsibility of correctly matching books to the library profile (usually by using a coding or classification device) and excluding inappropriate books. The library takes on a somewhat different responsibility of reviewing the vendor's work in light of the library collection and deciding, based on criteria that may or may not be codified, which books should be added to the collection. Selection takes place on two levels, the vendor and the library. It also needs to be pointed out that non-selection (i.e., not sending the book) is a function of the vendor only—the library cannot appraise or select what has not been sent. This is an often-ignored but important point. While vendors have little interest in establishing themselves as middlemen in the selection process for academic libraries,[2] they cannot help but do so with this type of approval plan.

Another less frequently-encountered type of approval plan is the publisher-based plan. One sees this type most frequently in the form of a plan for acquiring university press publications, although some libraries subscribe to this type of plan for commercial presses, or for specific areas of publishing such as art exhibition catalogs or music scores. In designing a publisher-based plan, the library and vendor agree on specific publishers for which publications will be provided. Certain non-subject parameters (such as cost or format) are agreed upon in advance but, in general, the library subscribes to the entire output of a specific press. The vendor once again is selecting books, albeit by an objective set of criteria. Having received the books, the library (quite unnecessarily) reviews and selects the titles appropriate to the collection, again using criteria which may or may not be universally agreed upon or understood within the library.

In the forms in which they are most commonly configured, the publisher-based model is the superior of the two plans for the academic library. There are many reasons for this. The first, and most important, is that the vendor selection criteria are utterly objective. A book either is or is not published by the University of Chicago Press, or by

Harper and Row, or by the Art Institute of Chicago, and that fact is evident to everyone involved. The level of continuing vendor decision-making could be considerably reduced when the plan is so designed.

Second, the publisher-based plan acknowledges what selectors already know (or should know), that some publishers are better than others when the research value of publications are considered. To illustrate this, in a library with a successful university press plan, one can review which titles are returned and why. Returns fall into two categories, that of duplicated titles and the very occasional inappropriate subject. University press titles in great part are of strong research value and meet the collection goals of an academic research library. Selectors can also make this same kind of determination with certain commercial presses. The art librarians will want Rizzoli publications, and the science librarians will purchase the Pergamon titles. It is very simple to test this by taking a current commercial publisher's catalog and checking the titles against the library's holdings. Certain presses will be collected in their entirety in one way or another. The most painless and efficient way to collect these titles is with a publisher-based approval plan. Without such a plan, the library and the vendor have to spend a considerable amount of time, money, and scarce staff resources to acquire titles one-by-one which will be wanted by the library anyway.

Third, a publisher-based plan provides a stage for rethinking how libraries use approval plans and how they affect the internal operation of an academic library. In order to decide this latter point, libraries must take the opportunity to clarify why an approval plan is necessary and what its effect is beyond the acquisition of materials.

Why do libraries use approval plans of any type? A frequently offered answer is that approval plans bring in essential and highly desirable books in the most cost-effective and efficient way. Approval plans are seen as aids to selection, giving librarians a book-in-hand opportunity to review current publications without committing themselves to a purchase. It is deemed to be a more efficient use of library staff than handling separate orders and invoices. Approval plan books should (and, for the most part, do) arrive more quickly than do books individually selected and ordered after a review is available. They can provide the core materials for an academic discipline, gathering in material around which more ephemeral titles can be collected. These are noble ideas all, but their implementation within the library may not stand up to close scrutiny. The notion of approval plans in their simplest form is a solid one: approval plans can bring in the best publications in an efficient manner. But do they? Many of the processes set up by both vendors and libraries contradict the basic idea behind approval plans.

Looking first at the vendor process for approval plans, one finds that vendors invest a sizeable amount of money in developing thesauri for approval profiles and in reviewing and coding each book. The Library of Congress classification scheme is used for coding both before the book arrives at the vendor and when it is in hand. In a sense, a capable approval plan vendor sets up a sophisticated subject cataloging section within the company and even provides the basic descriptive cataloging format in terms of edition, illustration, and sometimes even pagination. Whether a vendor simply uses CIP data without change or uses this data in tandem with some internal subject designation, there is expenditure in time and money by the vendor on behalf of the library. In addition, because the vendor is basing profile classification on the LC system, the very best service will only be as strong as the LC system, which is flawed. Any cataloger who uses this system will attest to its inconsistencies. A book on the political and economic structure of Latin America can have many homes in LC with oftentimes incompatible neighbors. This means, in a fair number of cases, that cross-disciplinary titles may not be sent on approval if one subject matches the profile and the other does not. If a library collects books on ethics but not on medicine, for example, and there is a book on medical ethics, there is no certainty the book will come on the approval plan. It can depend on how the book is classified by LC, how the vendor chooses to use this classification, and how carefully the profile is written.

In addition, there are no provisions for subjects that are not represented at the Library of Congress,[3] which seriously impedes the ability to describe and classify new subjects in a timely fashion. Even choosing another system, such as the Dewey Decimal Classification, does not raise the level of objectivity. This is especially true with a subject-based plan, where the proper subject descriptors will match a library profile with a book. This problem would, on the surface, appear to be nonexistent in a publisher-based profile, but in reality this does not seem to be the case. Vendors are most commonly set up to handle subject-based profiles as their first priority, and tend to process publisher-based books in the same manner.

Libraries currently subscribing to a publisher-based plan will see on slips accompanying the books the same data they would see were they to receive the book as a result of a subject profile. Because the notion of a publisher-based plan is different from that of a subject-based plan, there is little reason to treat these plans in the same way. Vendors could, if they were to rework some internal processes, simply identify a publication as belonging to the desired press and arrange for its shipment. This would circumvent the subject classification process and get the book to the library faster and cheaper. It is a more efficient use of resources and brings the vendor closer to the ideal of approval plans as being an efficient way of gathering in those publications which are commonly agreed to be the best.

Libraries are the main culprits in undermining some of the best reasons for approval plans. A fundamental attitude in academic libraries is the tendency to treat the approval plan as a bookstore. The word "approval" denotes that some decision has to be made on the part of the library to select or reject a book. This process often entails an elaborate sub-routine within an acquisitions department to deal with this selection. Typically, each approval shipment received by a library is displayed for a certain period of time to allow all selectors involved with the plan to review the books. This time period may last from a few days to a few weeks, depending upon the ability of selectors to view the books in a timely fashion. During the review period, selectors examine the books for their suitability for the collection. They may rely on requests for the book, on reviews, on their knowledge of the collection, or on instinct. Whatever forms the basis for a selection or rejection, the approval plan tends to serve the same purpose as a bookstore in which the owners (vendors) only display books they believe their customers will purchase. The only difference is that the activity takes place not in the bookstore (the vendor's office) but at home (in the library).

Two issues concerning the efficiency of the typical approval plan arise here. First, the selection period does not speed the books to their destination, which is the hands of the user. The books are tied up in various procedures and often their existence in the library is not known to the average library user. This latter problem can be circumvented by loading approval tapes into an online catalog. Second, reviewing and selecting such books seems to beg the question of the use of a librarian's time. It is helpful to ask how useful it is for the collection and for the library as a whole to have librarians reviewing and selecting approval books. If, in the case of a subject-based plan, a number of titles previously unknown to the selector are brought to his or her attention, one must question if that selector is spending his or her time appropriately.

A selector in an academic library should have a fairly complete knowledge of the mainstream publishing in his or her assigned discipline and should not have to rely upon the selection practices of the vendor. If this is not the case, and the subject-based plan is gathering in quantities of titles not previously identified by the selector, the selector should review his or her selection practices. In the case of publisher-based plans, the library already has clearly defined the presses it wants to receive, and for all intents and purposes the selection has been made. In neither case does it seem necessary for the selector to spend time in review of approval books. Yet, almost all libraries do this, thus slowing down the process of getting books to the user and spending professional abilities on the known instead of the unknown.

Our preoccupation with selecting the obvious is not unlike the development of cataloging within academic libraries in the past fifteen years. Previously, librarians were involved in all aspects of the cataloging operation, from establishing name and subject authorities to (in far too many cases) typing the cards for the catalog. As automated activities proceeded, more and more of the details of cataloging were relinquished to lower level staff or to the machine. Now, for the majority of us, the thought of a librarian cataloging from Library of Congress or CIP records would appear ludicrous and most certainly an inappropriate use of time and money. Those librarians concerned with the cataloging process know well what is needed to create a catalog record and have the confidence to give much of the non-professional work to their non-professional staff.

The librarians' input generally revolves around subject classification, quality control, or the establishing of new authority records. Our involvement with approval plans is parallel to, but lags behind, the development of cataloging procedures in that selectors still act as did the earlier catalogers. In many libraries, selectors are involved with the approval plan from the writing of the profile to the final selection or rejection of the book. It is not the approval process which is the problem, but the type of books to which it is applied.

To express it in concrete terms, all useful approval plans are going to bring in to the library those books with which selectors should be familiar in one form or another. Because of the economics of the marketplace, vendors will not be supplying (for example) esoteric association publications, pamphlets, or non-returnable titles on the approval plan. They will be supplying publications from commercial presses, known entities that are advertised and available. The vendor knows the marketplace, and a good vendor with a good profile (be it subject- or publisher-based) will bring in the known. As librarians, we are responsible for identifying the unknown and for using our knowledge of the disciplines we cover, the people we serve, and the lesser known non-commercial publishers and their publications and ephemera. By massive involvement with the approval plan—with selection and rejection and profile writing—we are sabotaging the good things which approval plans can bring us. The most central of these good things are the core books made available in the fastest and cost-effective way.

What approval plans have become, then, is a great idea whose ends and means have become somewhat snarled. If the goal of a good approval plan is to be "the firstest with the mostest," it needs to do three things: cut vendor cost and time (which could be reflected in higher discounts to libraries), cut library processing time (specifically review and selection time), and enhance professional involvement of librarians in the selection process. Doing this requires a rethinking of the approval process from beginning to end. There are a number of steps to re-creating a more positive approval process:

1. *Establish a publisher-based plan within the library*. This may be the university press plan well known to many libraries, or it could be extended to encompass commercial presses. A commercial press plan can work very well if the publishers are selected carefully. As previously suggested, this can be based on a review of library holdings from various presses. Also, many vendors are capable of providing quantitative lists of presses received on a subject-based plan, which will allow the library to see which presses are most often selected. Vendors are capable of making discriminations between parent and subsidiary presses or distribution houses. This facility gives libraries the opportunity to fine-tune the publication list so that unwanted publications from subsidiary presses can be kept from the publication profile.

The publisher-based profile is preferred because it is objective and therefore satisfying to, and efficient for, both the vendor and the library. One of the common complaints about a subject-based approval plan is the lack of forecasting ability by the library (and sometimes by the vendor as well). The built-in frustration of the subject-based plan is the continual question, "is it coming on the plan?" Vendors have tried to circumvent this problem by providing microfiche or other pre-shipment information, both of which are costly to the vendor and the library in both time and money. The publisher-based concept does much to alleviate this concern. If the profile is set up to receive, for example, Wiley Interscience publications, and the title the library desires is from that publisher, the book will come.

2. *The vendor needs to rework internal procedures*. In order to provide a high level of integrity and to satisfy the customer, vendors have developed relationships with publishers with care. In the larger com-

panies, vendors have publisher relations staff who work directly with publishers to ascertain what is coming out and to guarantee that the correct number of titles are shipped. In smaller companies, the contact with publishers may not be so structured, but the vendor, if it wishes to remain successful, will have established methods of obtaining publisher information. Using a publisher-based profile, a vendor could match publisher and profile without submitting titles to the time-consuming and rigorous profiling session which often occurs twice. This has the two advantages of reducing the vendor's overhead in profiling staff and shortening the time it takes to get a book to the library. Granted, the necessity for minor review of books for some libraries will still exist, for example those that do not wish to receive textbooks or reprints or some other format exclusion. Much of this review can take place when the title is first ordered by the vendor, obviating the need for even minimal review when the vendor's shipment is received.

3. *The library needs to rethink internal procedures.* These procedures are many and varied and include non-professional and professional procedures. First is a commitment by the selectors to the notion of a publisher-based plan, which carries with it the assurance that the desired publications will arrive in the library. This is more easily said than done in most settings. Again, the analogy of the selector and the cataloger arises: "will the OCLC catalog record be accurate enough?" becomes "will the vendor miss anything?" or "will the vendor send books we don't want?" The best, and maybe the only, way to become convinced of the objectivity and certainty of a publisher-based plan is to have one or to discuss experiences with libraries that have these kinds of plans, including university press plans.

Second, there has to be an agreement among selectors that the presses chosen are the presses wanted. Publisher-based plans do not work in any form if only some publications from a given press are wanted. One good way to analyze which additional presses are in demand is to receive notification slips for a few months from specific presses and review which are ordered heavily. Finally, the library needs to reorient its thinking to accept the approval plan books as it does continuations or standing orders. This notion is not new, but it has not been applied very seriously to approval plans. It was once common to have standing orders with several publishers to receive their publications; some academic libraries still handle university press publications in this way. Because the standing order books come into the library in a different way from approval books, however, they are thought of differently. In fact, acquiring approval books and standing order publications serves the same end and can be handled as the same process. In addition, the publisher-based approval plan parallels the vendor process, inasmuch as vendors, in establishing these publisher plans, are in fact establishing a standing order with the publisher on behalf of the library.

The effects are numerous and significant. Important books arrive more quickly and are processed more quickly within the library. Selectors are freed from routine selection activities to concentrate on identifying those materials which make each academic library so dynamic and special. The selector is concentrating his or her professional expertise in an area where it is really required. Our jobs are elevated in one more way with one more step.

What this in fact is calling for is something which was introduced several years ago by Richard Chapin. He noted that, among other things, approval plans tend to ignore the costs of selection within the library. It is not efficient to spend staff time in reviewing and selecting receipts. Costs for this review cannot be glossed over with higher discounts or with promises of getting material to the user more quickly.[4] The publisher-based "gathering plan," as it might be named, proves for a high level of control at a low cost to both the library and the vendor. The "approval plan," in contrast, affords several artificial controls which do not provide objectivity and so are not efficient. How does such a re-working affect organization within the library? It defines the comparative roles of the acquisitions unit and the selectors more clearly. Often, approval plans create overlaps in responsibilities among acquisitions librarians, selection librarians, and collection development librarians. Selectors expect that their disciplines have been adequately described to the vendor for the approval profile. The collection development librarian assumes that his or her wishes about reprints and costs of material are being carried out. The acquisitions librarian, serving as middleman with the vendor, hopes that he or she has provided all the correct words and phrases to the vendor to establish an adequate profile. Such overlaps in work create a high level of uncertainty and frustration for everyone involved, giving responsibility to many but not defining the base of authority for anyone. The gathering plan approach to approval plans ends much of this confusion, inasmuch as it reinforces the same guidelines that already exist for standing or blanket orders. The selectors are responsible for selecting the material, the collection development area is responsible for establishing the general guidelines for collecting, and the acquisitions unit is responsible for procuring it.

If approval plans are responsible for twenty percent of a library's domestic acquisitions, for example, then twenty percent of the work in selection and acquisition will be amalgamated with an already existing process. This obviously creates a streamlined and efficient organizational approach to the acquisition and selection of new domestic titles. In addition, revamping one area within acquisitions or within the selection process invariably leads to the rethinking of other procedures, a beneficial exercise which in the very least is a useful method of management review. A gathering plan approach to approval books also affects the way in which the budget is viewed and therefore treated. In many libraries the approval plan is an extra item, an expendable addition which can be deleted when the budget gets tight. It is not viewed as a means of bringing essential items into the library. A switch to a publisher-based gathering plan approach should change the way in which these core titles are viewed. It should also change the way in which the portion of the budget spent on the plan is treated.

As a case in point, when materials budgets are reduced, libraries generally approach the cancellation of standing orders with great caution. These standing orders involve a continued commitment on the part of the library to a series or set which cannot be broken lightly without affecting the quality of the collection. In a like manner, approval plan books should be viewed as representing essential items that need to be acquired by the library to maintain at least a modicum of collection integrity. It places these titles on the same priority level as continuations or periodicals. Since these approval books represent core items, they should be considered of equal importance. It also has the benefit of protecting the balance between money spent on monographs and on serial publications. As more and more materials money is spent on maintaining serial collections, there is a need within academic libraries as a whole to make a commitment to protecting the core of the monographs budget. One way of doing this is by treating the approval portion of the budget as if it were part of a continuing commitment. The gathering plan approach obviously accomplishes this, and it makes a statement in general about the importance of collecting essential monographs, even during times of relative poverty.

Professionalism is another area which is heavily influenced by this change in the handling of approval plans. The most obvious effect is on the activities of the selectors. Taking the same twenty percent acquisition of domestic books on approval, a selector should find that most of the time previously spent identifying, reviewing, selecting, and rejecting these titles can be spent with other assignments. There are undoubtedly some who will interpret this change in approval plans to mean an abdication of the responsibility for selection of material. However, this change does not free the selector from the responsibility of knowing about the publication of titles and being familiar with and conversant about new publications. *Selection* of titles is an activity very different from *review* of titles. Selection includes the highest level of professional activity: identification of the title; adequate knowledge of the subject, author, and/or publisher; knowledge of potential sources of review; knowledge of the users and their needs; and, possibly, information about acquiring the title.

Approval plans as they are normally constructed require selectors to do almost all of these activities on a continuing basis. In addition, subject-based plans require the selector to know, with some degree of accuracy, what has not been sent and to be able to evaluate it as well. The new approach to approval plans does not require this level of involvement by selectors, but it can, if desired, provide the opportunity for review of those titles that are known to be arriving. As with standing orders, the review can take place after the title is on the shelves. For the less fearful, or in libraries with enough resources to consider purchasing more than one copy, a review can take place at the point of receipt or through a circulating list.

The analogy of the catalog department of yesterday and today is appropriate. Unfortunately, as a profession we tend to review the tasks we handle only when economics or automation demand it. There is no pressing need to change our selection habits or to change approval plans that work adequately, and so they are not scrutinized. We need to force this self-examination upon ourselves, however, not only for the savings in time and money which it affords, but also for the development of the profession toward higher levels of achievement and personal accomplishment.

A rethinking of the treatment and place of approval plans within academic libraries will have several positive effects on the vendor, the librarian, the library budget, and the organization. Constant review of the processes which work in the library, such as approval plans, are as important to our growth as is the review and revamping of processes which have failed. One particular battle libraries will always fight is how to get the most to the user as fast as possible. A new approach to approval plans based on a gathering in of core publications can be a successful example of "the firstest with the mostest" strategy.

NOTES

1. Robert L. Chapman, ed. *New Dictionary of American Slang*. New York: Harper & Row, 1986, p. 135.

2. Hunter S. Kevil, "The Approval Plan of Smaller Scope," *Library Acquisitions: Practice and Theory* 9 (1985): 16.

3. A. C. Foskett, *The Subject Approach to Information*. 4th ed. London: Clive Bingley; Hamden, Connecticut: Linnet Books, 1982, p. 412.

4. Richard E. Chapin, "Summary Statement," in *Economics of Approval Plans: Proceedings of the Third International Seminar on Approval and Gathering Plans in Large and Medium Size Academic Libraries*, edited by Peter Spyers-Duran and Daniel Gore. Westport, Connecticut: Greenwood Press, 1972, pp. 120-121.

Analysis of Approval Plans
in ARL Libraries

Jean L. Loup

INTRODUCTION

Although many academic libraries use approval plans, questions about their value and possible long term effect continue to be asked. As early as 1970, Marion Wilden-Hart asked, "If a substantial number of larger libraries in the United States are using approval plans from a limited number of jobbers, are they all building up similar collections?"[1] Although expressing belief in the value of approval plans to provide a basic core, Wilden-Hart raised questions about their long-term effects and how to supplement approval plans to provide unique special collections.[2]

During the past fifteen years there have appeared in the literature a wide range of articles looking at approval plans and their use.[3] Early articles tended to be of a pro-or-con nature. By the mid-1970s the articles against the use of approval plans had disappeared and instead authors were treating the issue of effectiveness. Some wrote about the circumstances which lead to effective use; others studied vendor performance and choosing a vendor. None answered Wilden-Hart's question, "Are they all building up similar collections?"[4] and, a question for the late 1980s, if they are, is resource sharing at risk? This study attempts to answer these questions.

The study reported in this paper was funded by a Council on Library Resources Cooperative Research Grant for Librarians and Faculty Members. It has sought to learn the extent to which member institutions of the Association of Research Libraries (ARL) with Blackwell North America (B/NA) Approval Plans covering philosophy and political science are duplicating collections, and to find out what supplementary collection development practices are being used. By implica-

Jean L. Loup is Head, Documents Center and Senior Associate Librarian at the University of Michigan.

tion, the study also sought to examine the extent to which resource sharing was at risk as a result of approval plan use.

RESEARCH DESIGN

The study had two major objectives:

1. To compare approval plan profiles of selected libraries belonging to the Association of Research Libraries in order to determine whether they are building essentially duplicate collections through their approval plans.
2. To determine what methods and resources these selected research libraries are using in collection development to supplement approval plans for philosophy and political science.

To meet these objectives several research questions were developed:

— Are ARL libraries acquiring very similar collections as a result of using approval plans as the primary method of selection?
— What proportion of the currently-received materials are acquired through the approval plans and what through title-by-title selection?
— Do the selection patterns vary between the two subjects, philosophy and political science? In what ways?
— What methods and resources are being used by selected libraries to supplement their approval plans in the fields of philosophy and political science?

A decision was made to use Blackwell North America, Inc., as the approval plan vendor for the study because of the numeric coding for both subject and non subject descriptors which all libraries subscribing to the plan use to define their profiles, and because the company was known to be a major supplier of materials for academic libraries.

Since science has been considered by some as a less effective field in which to use approval plans as a major source of selection,[5] approval plan profiles for The University of Michigan Library for several subjects in the Humanities and in the Social Sciences were examined. Philosophy and political science were selected for the study because they represent manageable subjects for monitoring and reporting. In addition, they allowed us to study a subject in each of the major fields, Humanities and Social Sciences, for which approval plans have been most often recommended.[6] B/NA provided the investigators with a list of all ARL member libraries with B/NA approval plans which include philosophy and political science, a total of twenty-nine libraries.

The research was conducted in three stages, the first being a letter to the twenty-nine libraries, informing them about the study and requesting copies of their B/NA profiles. The second step was a questionnaire asking for data on expenditures, number of volumes purchased, size of collection, materials budget, and other similar data. Included with this mailing was a list of the questions which the investigators planned to ask during follow-up telephone interviews with the selectors involved. The third stage, the interviews, included an initial telephone call to schedule a time convenient for the collection development officer or selector to participate in a half-hour interview.

ANALYSIS OF B/NA PROFILES AND NSP'S

The initial letter was mailed in late July 1985 and replies from all twenty-nine libraries were received, a 100% response rate. One library wrote to say they had only a science profile, which reduced the population to twenty-eight libraries. By fall 1985, profiles were received from twenty-seven of these libraries; the twenty-eighth was received directly from B/NA in the summer of 1986.

Many of the respondents sent letters with thoughtful comments on the premise; some agreed and others did not, but all expressed a willingness to participate and an interest in the final results. The following is an excerpt from one of the letters:

> We use the approval plan to bring in the core, English language, contemporary materials, primarily to support undergraduate and graduate courses. The *real* difference between any two collections will most likely lie in the strategies used to bring in the other types of materials, e.g., foreign languages, esoteric publishers, formats, etc. The degree of activity in retrospective collection, or the strength that already exists in that category is also a critical factor to take into account.

As approval plan profiles arrived, both subject and non-subject parameters were examined; a decision was made to use "books" profiles only for each of the two subject fields, philosophy and political science. In most cases title difference was found in the subject choices made by the libraries in the study. All but six libraries chose to receive books for both philosophy and political science. Of the six which had exceptions to all books, four libraries had exceptions in one or the other of the two subjects, and two libraries had exceptions in both. For instance, one library chose books for all of philosophy except Arabic philosophy (15360413), Indic philosophy (15360430), and Other unspecified philosophical systems (15360490). Another eliminated Arabic philosophy, Asceticism (15360610), and Fate and fatalism (15360730) in philosophy, and Public administration (277856) in political science.

Blackwell/North American provides in its profiling not only the expected subject divisions and subdivisions, but also what they term non-subject parameters (NSP's), through which a library may choose Books, Forms, or None for items in divisions such as academic difficulty level, type of library, type of book, language of book, and type of publisher. An examination of the NSP's for the twenty-eight libraries in the study revealed some variations which might lead to differences in the library collections.[7]

Twenty-four of the 128 NSP's were designated as Book by all twenty-eight libraries. One additional NSP (trade publishing) was selected by twenty-seven, with the twenty-eighth library selecting none. Because the study had called for libraries using the approval plans in a comprehensive manner, the selections of this library (which uses the plan for university press titles only) have been eliminated from the NSP analysis.

The NSP's for which all libraries received books include the following:

    Academic difficulty level
        Professional books
        Other
    Readership level
        Specialist reader
        General reader
    Type of library
        University-research library
        Returnable-forms
    Type of book
        General book
        Multi-author text
    Type of edition
        Critical edition
        General edition
    Language of book
        English language

Type of publisher
    Trade publisher
Printing history
    New
Format of publication
    Hardbound book
Time characteristics of subject
    1900-1945
    20th century
    1945-1969
    1970 to future
    No time
Treatment of subject
    History of
    Political aspects
    Biographical treatment
    Social aspects of
    General or no specific treatment
    Psychological aspects of

On the other hand, a number of NSP's were chosen by one-third of the libraries or fewer. One library chose sixteen of these seldom-selected NSP's in the field of philosophy. The largest number of this group of NSP's chosen for political science was eleven, also by one library. The mode for both philosophy and political science is one and the median for both is two. Means (3.92 for philosophy and 3.43 for political science) are skewed for both subjects because a few libraries chose many of these NSP's. The five libraries which have chosen nine or more of these seldom-selected NSP's in their philosophy profiles and the five libraries which have chosen eight or more for their political science profiles are different in this respect from a large majority of the population.

The sixteen NSP's which were seldom selected seem to fall into three categories (1) *popular treatment and undergraduate level*; (2) *special formats*; and (3) *languages other than English*. No correlation was found between collection size or library expenditures and the decision to receive titles in any of the non-subject categories.

Most libraries selected the same level (book, form, or none) for both philosophy and political science, and for any one NSP the variation between the two subjects was never more than four libraries. Most typically, the variation was one or two libraries. Occasionally the variation can be explained by the differences in the two subjects, such as that in NSP's 522 (Data book/tables) and 523 (Atlas); at other times the only explanation seems to be the expected variations among libraries.

Because the profiles for these subjects were always part of a more comprehensive profile (often a humanities profile or a social sciences profile), there are occasional oddities, such as NSP 534 (Musical scores) for which eight libraries chose books in philosophy and seven in political science. NSP 801 (English as the language of the original) was chosen by twenty-five libraries as books for philosophy and by twenty-six as books for political science. Although B/NA distributed no titles in that category during 1985/86, it is likely that libraries are seldom interested in translations of works published originally in English. The libraries which selected forms for NSP 901 (University press) have separate approval plans for university press titles with another vendor.

The one NSP for which the selection pattern seems destined to change is NSP 1116 (Software), eight libraries having chosen forms in 1985 and nineteen none. Most libraries, in the interviews conducted later, indicated that they had begun to collect in this area.

During 1985/86 B/NA distributed more than 20,000 titles profiled for five NSP's: University/research library; general edition; English language; hardbound; and general or no specific treatment. In addition, between 5000 and 20,000 titles were profiled for another nine NSP's; these were professional book, other book, specialist reader, general reader, undergraduate library, general book, paperbound, 1970 to future, and no time. For these NSP's all libraries chose books except for undergraduate library and paperbound. For the former, two libraries chose forms, the rest books; for the latter one library chose forms for political science only; the rest chose books.

In contrast the eighteen NSP's for which fewer than fifty titles were profiled have a wide variation in selection patterns. None was selected as books by all libraries, although two came within two libraries. The number of libraries selecting these NSP's as books ranged from zero to twenty-six.

In addition to the NSP's, B/NA provides the capability of limiting the price of a title to be distributed on approval. Among the libraries in this study, there is a wide range of upper limits, from $60 to $200. Below that price, the library will accept books; above it the library wants forms. Some libraries also set lower limits, that is, below a certain price, B/NA should send forms or nothing. Only three libraries differentiated between the dollar limits set for philosophy and those set for political science. There appeared to be no correlation between size of library and the amount of dollar limit.

ANALYSIS OF QUESTIONNAIRE RESPONSES

Twenty-five libraries answered a questionnaire with numerical data on approval plan purchasing, collection size and materials budget. As the responses and the initial tabulation were examined, it became clear that variations in the kind of records kept and the unit of measurement reported were considerable. Although the expectation had been to concentrate on comparisons of philosophy and political science, data were not consistently available. In most cases, therefore, the findings are reported on all purchases and returns rather than for the two subject fields compared by approval plan profile. In addition, information reported on size of collection and expenditures for materials varied from published statistics for ARL libraries in several cases. In order to make comparisons among all libraries in the study the decision was made to use published statistics when these varied from the numerical data recorded on the questionnaire.

Tabulation of data from questionnaire responses was made separately for those libraries which reported on the basis of main library only and those libraries which reported for a total library system.

Size of library collection appeared to be the most useful basis for making comparisons; however, promised anonymity for libraries in the study was an important consideration. A decision was made to group libraries into three categories by size of collection in 1984-85; Category I libraries had over three million volumes, Category II libraries had two to three million volumes, and Category III libraries had one to two million volumes. These categories have been used throughout the report.

Expenditures for B/NA Approval Purchases

Table 1 shows the total B/NA expenditures, percent of total expenditures for materials, number of titles purchased through B/NA approval, and size of collection category (I-III) for the sixteen libraries which reported information on B/NA approval plan activity on the basis of the total library system. Table 2 provides the same information for the nine libraries which reported for the main library.

Each of the two major groups (systems or main library only) had one or more of each collection size category represented. Among the total library systems (Table 1), both the largest amount ($312,644)

Table 1.   EXPENDITURES AND PURCHASES BY LIBRARIES
            REPORTING FOR TOTAL LIBRARY SYSTEMS

B/NA Expend.	% of Total Expend.	Titles Purchased B/NA	Coll. Size Category
312,644	11.1	12.209	III
300,000	8.8	10,200	II
225,000	13.7	6,635	III
212,013	6.2	7,129	II
211,116	4.9	8,148	I
208,046	8.5	6,935	II
195,103	3.4	6,033	I
191,548	9.0	7,396	II
182,447	8.3	6,329	III
178,333	9.4	6,907	II
173,600	5.9	7,703	II
145,534	3.4	5,942	I
145,000	7.3	5,400	III
120,435	8.5	4,493	III
116,018	2.7	4,098	I
65,329	2.7	2,345	II

and the largest percent of total budget for materials (13.7%) were spent by libraries of one to two million volumes. The range for total B/NA expenditures was $65,329 to $312,644. Range in percent of total expenditures for B/NA approval purchases was 2.7% to 13.7%.

Among the Main Library Only group (Table 2), one library with a collection of two to three million volumes (Category II) had both the largest expenditure ($249,449) and largest percent of total materials expenditure (12.2%). A Category I library (over three million volumes) had both the smallest B/NA expenditure ($56,858) and the smallest percent of total materials expenditure for B/NA approval purchases (1.2%) Range for total B/NA expenditures was $56,858 to

Table 2.   EXPENDITURES AND PURCHASES BY LIBRARIES
           REPORTING FOR MAIN LIBRARY ONLY

B/NA Expend.	% of Total Exp.	Titles Pur. B/NA	Coll. Size Category
249,449	12.2	8,177	II
218,853	8.3	8,219	III
200,840	5.4	7,004	III
199,000	7.2	7,384	III
195,934	9.9	5,810	III
137,322	7.6	5,845	III
117,464	5.5	4,720	III
111,939	4.3	5,041	II
56,858	1.2	2,394	I

$249,449. The range in percent of total expenditures for B/NA was 1.2% to 12.2%.

As would be expected, there was considerable variation from the smallest number of titles purchased to the largest number (2,345 to 12,209 in the Total Library Systems group, and 2,394 to 8,177 in the Main Library Only group). There is also variation in the average cost per title, based on the B/NA expenditures for a library and the number of titles purchased; e.g., one library from Table 2 spent $195,934 for 5,810 titles, an average of $33.72 per title, and another spent $137,322 for 5,845 titles, an average of $23.50 per title. This may be due to several factors. The library with the smaller cost per book had a greater return rate and also included more "form" and fewer "book" choices in its NSP profile. The library with the larger cost per book may have included other more costly subject categories in its approval plan. These factors were not examined for the current study.

Range and Mean of Collection Size, Materials Budget, and B/NA and B/NA Expenditures by Three Size Categories

Table 3 shows the range and mean size of three groups of ARL libraries included in the study. The five libraries in Category I range in size of collection from approximately three to six million volumes in 1985, according to ARL published statistics. The average (mean) size

Table 3   SUMMARY DATA BY CATEGORIES

Coll. Size Category	No. of Libraries	Range Vol.	Mean Size	Range of Budget	Mean Budget	Range B/NA Expend.	Mean B/NA Expend.	% of Mean Budget on B/NA
I	5	3-6 mil.	4,809,814	4,256,069-5,754,736	4,663,576	56,858-211,116	144,926	3.1%
II	10	2-3 mil.	2,214,665	1,894,874-3,406,656	2,543,371	65,329-300,000 *	187,806 *	7.4% *
III	13	1-2 mil.	1,584,196	1,416,294-3,703,014	2,369,469	120,435-312,644 **	186,813 **	7.9% **

* Based on 9 libraries reporting

** Based on 11 libraries reporting

36

of libraries in this category was 4,809,814. The annual budget for materials in these libraries ranged from $4,256,069 to $5,754,736 with a mean of $4,663,576. Expenditures for materials purchased on a B/NA Approval Plan ranged from $56,858 to $211,116; mean expenditures for these five libraries was $144,926. Percent of the group's mean budget for materials spent on B/NA approval purchase was only 3.1%.

The ten libraries in collection size Category II ranged from two to three million volumes in 1985; mean size was 2,214,665 volumes. Materials budget for these libraries ranged from $1,894,874 to $3,406,656 with a mean of $2,543,371. B/NA approval purchases ranged from $65,329 to $300,000; mean B/NA expenditure was $187,806 for this group, 7.4% of their mean budget for materials. It should be noted that B/NA expenditures for Category II were based on nine libraries which reported this information.

The largest group of the ARL libraries in the study was collection size Category III, thirteen libraries which ranged in size from one to two million volumes in 1985. Mean size of these library collections was 1,584,196. Category III libraries has annual budgets for materials of $1,416,294 to $3,703,014; mean of the group's materials budget was $2,369,469. Expenditures for material purchases through B/NA purchases was 7.9%. (B/NA expenditure figures were based on information from the eleven libraries reporting.)

Both B/NA expenditures and percent of their total mean budget spent on the B/NA Approval Plan were less for the largest libraries (Category I) in this study than for either of the other groups. Percent of expenditures for the group of libraries in Category I was less than half that of Category III libraries as a group. On the other hand, libraries as grouped in Categories II and III were not very different from each other. Category II had a mean of approximately $1000 more than Category III although Category III devoted a slightly larger portion of their aggregate budget on B/NA approval purchases than did Category II, 7.9% for the former to 7.4% for the latter.

None of these ARL Libraries is small; all had 1985 collections of more than one million volumes and budgets for materials of more than one million dollars. It appears, however, that the larger libraries are spending a proportionately smaller amount of their materials budgets on the B/NA Approval Plan than the other libraries studied. It also appears that there is little difference between libraries in the other two categories in terms of amount spent on B/NA Approval Plans.

B/NA Returns

Table 4 shows the number and percent of books returned to B/NA by each of the twenty-five libraries from which questionnaire responses were received. While there is considerable variation overall, the greatest variation, both in percent and number of returns, is found in Category III. Here the smallest percent of returns (.2%) and the largest (29.4%) are found. In actual numbers the range is 12 to 1872.

Second in number of returns (1,595) was the library which received the largest number of titles on approval from B/NA (13,804). This library also purchased the greatest number of titles (12,209 as shown in Table 4). No correlation was found between collection size category and percent or number of returns.

Sixteen libraries reported that they kept records of the books returned and the nature of those returns on their B/NA Approval Plans. Nine libraries did not keep such records at the time of the survey (Fall, 1985) although one reported an intention to do so in the future. Three libraries did not respond to the questionnaire. Three major reasons were given for returning books: (1) duplicates (most frequently mentioned); (2) defective copies; and (3) rejections because of subject, treatment, or format.

Number of books returned on an approval plan, reasons for returning them, and use made of records of returns varied considerably among the libraries in this study. While some librarians believed that these records could help in collection management, others did not think that the possible gains would be sufficient to warrant the time expenditure involved.

Other Approval Plans Used

Twenty-five libraries responded to the question "What other approval plans which you use in addition to B/NA would cover philosophy and political science?" The number reported ranged from twenty-two for one library to zero for four libraries. The mean was 2.96, somewhat skewed by the one library with twenty-two. Both median and mode were two. Approval plans mentioned in addition to the B/NA plan included both foreign and U.S. vendors. The data indicate that four of the five largest libraries have five or more approval plans, but among the other two groups there does not appear to be any difference attributable to size.

The eight other approval plan vendors which were reported by three or more of the twenty-five libraries are B.H. Blackwell, Harrassowitz, Touzot, Yankee Book Peddler, Casalini Libri, African Imprint and

Table 4.   B/NA RETURNS

Coll. Size Category	% of Return	Number Returned	Number Received
I	14.2	983	6,925
I	13.4	1,266	9,414
I	12.6	871	6,904
I	7.8	203	2,597
I	7.6	337	4,435
II	16.5	1,374	8,309
II	11.7	944	8,073
II	10.7	888	8,284
II	8.6	722	8,425
II	7.3	540	7,447
II	7.2	788	10,988
II	5.8	310	5,351
II	3.0	75	2,420
II	.8	63	8,240
III	29.4	1,872	6,365
III	18.1	1,200	6,600
III	11.7	627	5,347
III	11.6	1,595	13,804
III	10.1	748	7,383
III	6.3	390	6,235
III	4.9	329	6,658
III	4.6	354	7,738
III	3.7	223	6,033
III	2.7	196	7,200
III	.2	12	8,231

Puvill. Since all but one of these approval plans supply books from one or more foreign countries (a number of other plans listed by one or two libraries do this also), their use would be likely to limit the foreign book purchases from B/NA for some of the libraries in the study. The one United States based vendor, Yankee Book Peddler, was used by four libraries primarily to obtain books from various American university presses. This also would represent a limitation on the B/NA profiles for these four libraries.

INTERVIEW RESPONSES

To obtain the information on supplementary collection practices in participating libraries, telephone interviews were planned with the collection development officer. In some cases two or more interviews for a library were arranged and held with selectors in order to get information about collection practices in both philosophy and political science. All twenty-eight libraries were reached through this process. From the information received in the interviews the distinct differences which make each of the libraries unique began to appear.

Languages

Only one library indicated it did no foreign language selection. In the others the larger the library the more likely it is to be selecting more languages; the four largest libraries indicated they collect in all languages. European languages are the most commonly selected; there is more interest in collecting in Asian languages than in Middle Eastern languages.

Non-trade Publishing

Collection of non-trade publications appears to be somewhat related to size of total collection. The largest libraries in the study more often reported collecting extensively in materials from non-trade publishers; this was especially notable in society publications. The smallest libraries were more likely than others in the study to report that they did limited collection or that they rarely or never collected from these sources. Strong collections in special areas or of one type of private publishing were reported by research libraries of every size in the study. Overall, private publishing is acquired more often and more extensively in political science than in philosophy.

Formats Selected

Each of the twenty-eight libraries in the study were asked to identify the formats other than books in which they collected materials on philosophy and on political science. As one would expect, all twenty-eight libraries collect serials for both disciplines, philosophy and political science. In general, libraries reported collecting more formats for political science than for philosophy. The greatest difference between the two disciplines was in the number of libraries collecting maps, twenty in political science and only four in philosophy, but that variation was hardly surprising. Several libraries reported that audiovisual materials for instruction and electronic data bases, (e.g., ICPSR data tapes in political science and Thesaurus Lingua Grecia data base in philosophy) were administered outside the library. Some noted that they were developing policies to expand the formats in which they would collect, especially in the area of computer software. One collection development officer responded that selection is "format blind" in theory; the policy in that library is to collect research materials regardless of format. On the whole, the largest libraries collect in a greater variety of formats than either the libraries of two to three million volumes or those with one to two million volumes. Size of collection appears to be related to number of formats in a collection.

Retrospective Purchasing

While only one of the libraries indicated no retrospective activity, several others indicated limited involvement. Whether a library engages in such purchasing or not depends on several factors: the strength of the existing collection, the interest of the faculty, the money available for such purchases, and the time available to search out needed titles. One selector believes online access will enhance his ability to do retrospective purchasing.

Standing Orders

While twenty-three of the twenty-eight libraries have standing orders in both subjects, the five remaining libraries indicated some level of limitation on such orders. There is only a slight relationship between the use of standing orders and the size of the library.

Resource Sharing

Fifteen libraries, of the twenty-eight, indicate that they participate in resource sharing agreements, ten others in a limited way, and three not at all. Fourteen libraries are members of the Center for Research Libraries while two others indicate they withdrew two years ago. Two of the fourteen indicated withdrawal is under consideration. There are nine members of the Research Libraries Group (three others have joined since the interviews were conducted). A number of regional arrangements were identified.

There seems to be a reasonable commitment to the concept of resource sharing, although no indication to what extent participating in such an agreement affects the actual selection of materials. (In the future, studies such as RLG's "Conoco Study" may shed light on this issue.)

Analysis of Interlibrary Loan

Twelve libraries indicate they have an active program for reviewing interlibrary loan requests and ten others do something but do not have an active program. The remaining six have no program. Libraries in Category III are more likely to engage in analysis of interlibrary loans than libraries in Categories I and II.

Exchange and Gift Programs

The Category I libraries are more likely to have both an exchange program and an active gift-seeking program than the libraries in either Category II or Category III.

Collection Evaluation/Assessment Activity

Only one library, a Category III library, indicated collection evaluation and assessment are primary activities, although most others are actively involved in some evaluation or assessment project. Only two libraries, one from Category II, the other from Category III, reported no such activity. The most frequently mentioned activities included the National Collections Inventory Project, the RLG members' Conspectus work, and the national shelflist measurement. Other activities mentioned were the development of collection policy statements, checking bibliographies, and storage review. Several librarians noted the importance of faculty contact and involvement, especially during times of serials cancellations.

One selector speculated that the advent of the online catalog will have a major impact on the selector's ability to do collection evaluation and assessment.

Preservation Activity

Although several libraries indicated they have no formal preservation program, all identified the presence of some preservation activity.

Time Spent by Selectors

Percent of time spent on selection in each of the two subject areas studied varied greatly. During the interviews twenty-five respondents gave an estimate of time spent on selection in each of the two fields studied; three libraries reported that 50% or more of a selector's time was spent on philosophy, and three (not the same libraries) reported that 50% or more time was spent on selecting materials in political science. Most libraries reported spending considerably less time in selecting materials for either field, however. The mode category for both fields and the median category for political science was 20-29% of a selector's time. The median category for philosophy was even less, 10-19% of a selector's time.

As reported for the libraries in this study, the larger libraries showed the least variation in time allocated for selection in the two subject fields; the smaller research libraries (Category III) showed both the most variation and the greatest amount of time spent, on average.

SUMMARY AND CONCLUSIONS

The study had two major objectives: (1) To compare approval plan profiles of selected ARL libraries to determine whether they are building essentially duplicate collections through their approval plans, and (2) To determine what methods and resources these selected research libraries are using in collection development to supplement approval plans for philosophy and political science.

Twenty-eight libraries with Blackwell North America approval plans which included philosophy and political science constituted the population of the study. Profiles with subject and non-subject parameters covering the two subjects were received for all libraries, and one or more respondents from each library participated in a telephone interview. Twenty-five libraries answered a questionnaire with numerical data on approval plan purchasing, collection size and materials budget.

Conclusions, which are limited to the libraries in this population, are presented with the key questions which have guided our research:

(1) Are ARL libraries acquiring very similar collections as a result of using approval plans as the primary method of selection?

It was determined early in the project that there were very few differences in the subject profiles among libraries in the study; philosophy is usually covered by the general humanities profile, and political science by the general social science profile.

An examination of the number of titles profiled by B/NA for each non-subject parameter (NSP) reveals two points: (1) all libraries in the study selected books for the NSP's with the most titles profiled; and (2) the variation in their receipts of the NSP's less frequently selected applies to many fewer titles. Both points support the conclusion that the libraries are receiving very similar collections through their B/NA approval plans.

(2) What proportion of the currently-received materials is acquired through the approval plans and what through title-by-title selection?

Although the amount and percentage of B/NA approval plan purchases varied among the twenty-five libraries for which numerical data was received, the largest percentage of a library's total expenditure was 13.7. The percentage of the mean budget spent on B/NA purchases by collection size category was: Category I (over 3 million volumes) 3.1%; Category II (2 to 3 million volumes) 7.4%; and Category III (1 to 2 million volumes) 7.9%.

Information on title-by-title (firm order) purchases by the libraries in the study was not available for comparison, but one librarian reported: "The titles we acquire through B/NA represent less than half of the titles we acquire for these subject areas — many more titles are acquired via firm order."

(3) Do the selection patterns vary between the two subjects, philosophy and political science? In what ways?

Overall, there is little variation in the patterns of use of the NSP's for the two subjects, and when it does exist, it seems logically based in the subject. For example, more libraries selected books for the NSP for atlases in political science than in philosophy, and more libraries selected books for the NSP's that relate to early time periods for philosophy than for political science.

For most activities which supplement the approval plans discussed during the interviews, libraries tend to have system-wide programs that affect both subjects. Two exceptions were in the patterns of selection of non-trade publishing and in the formats other than books acquired. In both cases materials in political science were acquired more extensively than those in philosophy.

Some variation was found in the allocation of selector's time for philosophy and for political science. The median time category for selectors in philosophy was 10 to 19% while the median for selectors in political science was 20 to 29%.

(4) What methods and resources are being used by selected libraries to supplement their approval plans in the fields of philosophy and political science?

Libraries in the study reported purchasing by firm order and standing order, acquiring materials through gifts and exchange and through shared resources. They are using retrospective purchasing, analysis of interlibrary loans, collection evaluation and assessment techniques, and are acquiring many formats and non-trade publications often not available on approval plan. In general, the larger the library the more the library reported supplementary activities, but in the case of analysis of interlibrary loan, the smallest libraries did more analysis than the larger ones.

Libraries are collecting widely in foreign languages, but the largest libraries tend to include any language which is appropriate to their collection. For the smaller libraries, European languages are the most common with Asian languages selected more than Middle Eastern.

Preservation as a collection management activity is now established as appropriate. All libraries indicated some level of activity. The role of the selector in the process is, however, less well defined.

General Conclusions

The libraries in this study appear to be using approval plans to meet the needs of their institutions' curriculum and to acquire core collections. Some are using many approval plans while others are not. There is a variety as revealed in the supplementary collection activities reported. Size of collection and size of materials budget appear to be related to the breadth of variety reported; the larger the library budget and the larger the library collection, the broader the selection activity.

Although there seems to be a reasonable commitment to the concept of resource sharing, it tends to occur at the regional level more frequently than at the national level. There appears to be no correlation between the size of library and the extent to which the library participates in such programs.

Extending research library collections to include new formats, e.g., computer software and electronic data bases, was discussed by a number of collection development officers during our interviews with them. A study similar to this one done three to five years from now would undoubtedly reveal more formats as well as more cooperative collection development.

Throughout much of the country, the impact of a declining economy on collection development was evident. Materials budgets have suffered while costs of publications needed by the research community continue to increase. In many cases staff reductions have made it impossible to use some of the strategies recognized by our respondents as important collection maintenance activities, e.g., monitoring ILL, doing retrospective purchasing, assessing the collection systematically, and planning for resource sharing. Approval plans are providing a lifeline for some libraries in which selectors' time is minimal or even nonexistent.

We are no longer concerned that libraries are building up similar collections through the use of approval plans nor are we concerned that resource sharing is at risk. We do believe that continued efforts to individualize activities must be maintained and increased whenever possible. Further study of the specific sources used for this purpose, as suggested by one respondent, is planned.

NOTES

1. Wilden-Hart, Marion. "The Long-Term Effects of Approval Plans." *Library Resources & Technical Services* 14 (Summer 1970): 403.

2. *Ibid.*, 400-406.

3. A more extensive review of the literature will be found in the authors' grant report, *Comparison of Approval Plan Profiles and Supplementary Collection Development Activities in Selected ARL Libraries.* November 1986. (submitted to ERIC in January 1987).

4. Wilden-Hart. "Long-Term Effects." p. 403.

5. Evans, G. Edward, and Claudia White Argyres. "Approval Plans and Collection Development in Academic Libraries." *Library Resources & Technical Services* 18 (Winter 1974): 50; Axford, H. William. "Approval Plans: An Historical Overview and an Assessment of Future Value." In *Shaping Library Collections for the 1980's,* edited by Peter Spyers-Duran and Thomas Mann, Jr. 8. Phoenix, Oryx Press, 1980.

6. Axford, *Ibid.*

7. A complete report of the selections of NSP's for the libraries in this study will be found in "Appendix D: Selections of the Non-Subject Parameters" in the authors' grant report, *Comparison of Approval Plan Profiles.*

BIBLIOGRAPHY

Axford, H. William. "Approval Plans: An Historical Overview and an Assessment of Future Value." In *Shaping Library Collections for the 1980's*, edited by Peter Spyers-Duran and Thomas Mann, Jr. Phoenix, Oryx Press, 1980.

Evans, G. Edward, and Claudia White Argyres. "Approval Plans and Collection Development in Academic Libraries." *Library Resources & Technical Services* 18 (Winter 1974): 35-50.

Snoke, Helen Lloyd, and Jean L. Loup. *Comparison of Approval Plan Profiles and Supplementary Collection Development Activities in Selected ARL Libraries*. November 1986. (submitted to ERIC in January 1987).

Wilden-Hart, Marion. "The Long-Term Effects of Approval Plans." *Library Resources & Technical Services* 14 (Summer 1970): 400-406.

Up the Elevator:
An Examination
of Approval Plan Inflation
and Its Impact on Libraries

Dana Alessi

Item: "Higher education systems in twenty states . . . have already been forced to make budget cuts in the midst of the current fiscal year . . . [S]tates have less money on hand now than they did six years ago."[1]

Item: "On May 21 the Dallas City Council accepted a 3% cut in the Dallas Public Library budget . . . In slicing $496,000 from its $16.5 million budget . . . the library cancelled the purchase of 20,000 books."[2]

Item: "The University of Texas at Austin will spend 15% ($200,000) less this year than last, partly because of increases in foreign serials subscriptions, the decline of the dollar, and the growing proportion of the budget spent on foreign publications. The reduction reflects an overall cut of $14 million in University spending."[3]

Item: "[Was 1986] a healthy overall market for trade books? Not really . . . It sometimes seemed . . . that more copies were being sold of far fewer books, and that the book business was moving closer to the boom-or-bust mentality of Broadway or the movies . . . [T]here were signs of shrinkage in the trade business. Macmillan announced heavy future list cutting . . . and Arbor House also said it would prune its list by nearly 50% within two years."[4]

Peruse any of the current journal literature in higher education, publishing, or librarianship, and one will find similar article after article

Dana Alessi is Director of Monographic and Selection Services at Blackwell North America.

on shrinking higher education budgets, stagnant or declining library budgets, and a generally lackluster publishing performance. Couple this with articles on soaring journal inflation, differential pricing, and the declining dollar, and the evidence indicates that, to paraphrase, library materials prices are going up by the elevator and library budgets are going up (or, in some cases, down) by the stairs. Clearly, this is not the best of times to be a librarian or, even worse, a library bookseller.

As a book vendor, I am acutely aware of the emphasis increasingly being placed on serials in the average academic library. The *Bowker Annual* statistics for academic library acquisitions expenditures reflect the decline in the percentage of library materials budgets being spent on books (from 51.7% in 1982-83 to 49% in 1983-84), the corresponding increase in serials budgets (from 37.7% to 39%) and a substantial increase in microform expenditures from 0.9% to 1.6%.[5]

While libraries have committed ever larger chunks of their materials budgets to serials over the past few years, American book title production by and large increased through 1983, although it has been dropping since (Table 1). However, if other approval book vendors have the same experience as Blackwell North America, the number of titles treated on approval plans has grown (Table 2) and although inflation has not been running as rampant as in the early 1980s, nevertheless prices of books have steadily crept upward. Additionally, faculty have not lessened their requests for books.

Thus, librarians face a quandary — how to stretch straining materials

TABLE 1

AMERICAN BOOK TITLE PRODUCTION, 1980-1985

All Hard & Paper

1980	42377
1981	48793
1982	46935
1983	53380
1984	51058
1985	50070

Sources: Bowker Annual   and Publishers' Weekly

TABLE 2

TITLES TREATED ON THE BLACKWELL NORTH AMERICA
APPROVAL PLAN, 1980-1986*

	NEW	REPRINT	TOTAL
1979/1980	21626	2009	23635
1980/1981	22413	1724	24137
1981/1982	23827	864	24691
1982/1983	25112	676	25788
1983/1984	26983	819	27802
1984/1985	28528	779	29307
1985/1986	28914	932	29846

*Excludes serial titles treated Standing Order Only.

budgets for maximum effectiveness. Publisher-based approval plans are one method to alleviate pressures on the approval budget as well as providing an accurate monitoring tool; approval plans have been under additional scrutiny for subject and non-subject parameter belt-tightening. In addition, librarians have been closely following fluctuations of the dollar and have become much more aware of the value of purchasing titles from country of origin where almost assuredly a better book bargain will result. Book vendors have been pressured to give higher discounts, shrinking their already slim operating margins. Serials lists have been analyzed for possible cancellations, and many libraries have taken a hard line toward placement of new subscriptions and continuations.

Herbert White, for one, has decried the tendency of library administrators to minimize the impact of shrinking materials budgets by cancelling duplicates, ceasing to place new subscriptions and shifting funds from monographs to serials. Shifting funds from monographs to the serials budget, he states,

> is a con game, but it is a self-deception. The nonrenewal of serials subscriptions represents a highly visible action. The decision to cut the monographic budgets affects an as-yet-unidentified and even perhaps not-yet-published book. What we don't know can't hurt us. Except, of course, that it does, particularly if applied across the board within the library budget. There are subject dis-

ciplines, particularly in the humanities, which are far more dependent on monographs than on serials. . . . [The] tactic must
certainly end some time. If present trends were extended, by
1990 major academic libraries would be buying no new monographs whatsoever.[6]

Although White urged selective cuts, for the most part, libraries are
still making cuts across the board on approval plans without always
analyzing by subject discipline. It is simply easier to apply one simple
general cost-cutting strategy (e.g., cutting the price limit on all approval titles by $10.00) rather than individual subjects due to limited
comparative price data. Although the Bowker price statistics can be
useful, they do not always represent the materials an academic library
buys. There is little other comparative price data available. Indeed, in
an article written in 1982, Frederick Lynden pointed out the need for
accurate academic materials cost data and the lack of information on
prices.[7]

In considering materials costs, inflation, and the impact on libraries, vendors, and publishers, I found several unanswered questions and several hypotheses to test. First, has university press publishing increased or decreased during the 1980s? How have university
press prices fared when compared to the average book prices?

Second, what are the output and price trends for selected disciplines
in the humanities, social sciences, and sciences? Are art books still
expensive and religion books still cheap? How has reliance on journals
affected science disciplines?

Finally, what are the price and output trends for foreign titles distributed in the U.S.? How can this information assist librarians in
budgeting and planning?

Since 1975-76, Blackwell North America has annually published its
Approval Program Coverage & Cost Study, showing average prices
for all books treated on the approval plan as well as university presses.
The data for costs are broken down by the primary four digit subject
codes assigned to each book treated on the approval plan.

In 1985, Blackwell North America treated approximately 30,000
new titles on its approval plan, or about 60% of total book output.
Since the Blackwell North America approval plan excludes juveniles,
mass market paperbacks, subsequent serial volumes (annuals, year-
books, etc.), high school textbooks, pro forma titles, and extremely
popular trade books, the Approval Program Coverage & Cost Study
can be used as a relatively reliable tool for academic book price infor-

mation for academic libraries, especially for those libraries seeking a handle on approval program costs.

One caution is in order, however. Until the 1978-79 figures which are included in the 1979-80 Coverage & Cost Study, Blackwell North America cited a net price figure, factored according to a formula predicated on a typical discount from list price. Thus, for true comparative purposes, that data is not meaningful, and any study using the Blackwell North America Coverage and Cost Study must begin with the 1978-79 data for an accurate comparison. My comments will be based on 1979-80 and subsequent data.

Table 3 shows the average price of a book treated on the Blackwell North America approval plan since 1979-80, as well as the percentage increase from the previous year. Inflation has moderated substantially from the double-digit increases of the early 1980s.

It would appear, from this data, that the average inflation rate can be predicted to run about 4% for the remainder of 1986-87 and well into 1987-88.

The Blackwell North America data does not compare particularly well with the Bowker data for approximately the same period (Table 4). It should be remembered, however, that the Bowker data is limited to hardcover output only, whereas the Blackwell North America data considers both hard and soft cover, as well as those titles more suited to academic library selection.

Table 5 analyzes university press output and the average cost and increase for 1979-86. Perhaps the most startling aspect of these figures is the increase in the number of university press titles published, a 37.5% increase since 1979-80 compared with a 26.3% overall increase in the number of titles treated on the Blackwell North America approval plan. Thus, a library wishing to collect university presses comprehensively and inclusively needs 87.5% additional dollars than it did in 1979-80.

As can be seen from Figure 1, the actual gap between the price of the average book and a university press book has actually begun to widen at the same time university press publication has seemingly exploded.

Several reasons may account for increased publication and more slowly rising prices than trade presses:

1. Subsidization.

Because university presses are subsidized by their institutions, they can keep their unit costs lower, even though print runs may be small.

2. The "bottom" line.

This is quite the opposite of subsidization but, as many institutional

TABLE 3

AVERAGE BLACKWELL NORTH AMERICA APPROVAL BOOK PRICE,
1979-1986

	PRICE	PERCENT INCREASE OVER PREVIOUS YEAR
1979-1980	$22.37	+13.6%
1980-1981	25.42	+13.6%
1981-1982	28.05	+10.3%
1982-1983	29.14	+ 3.9%
1983-1984	30.13	+ 3.4%
1984-1985	30.13	+ 0.0%
1985-1986	32.43	+ 7.6%
1986-1987 (6 months)	33.19	+ 2.3%

TOTAL INCREASE 1979-1980/1985-1986 = 45%

TABLE 4

U.S. HARDCOVER BOOKS: AVERAGE PRICES, 1980-1985

	AVERAGE PRICE	PERCENT INCREASE/DECREASE OVER PREVIOUS YEAR
1980	$24.64	
1981	26.63	+ 8.0%
1982	30.34	+13.9%
1983	31.19	+ 2.8%
1984	29.99	- 3.8%
1985	31.46	+ 4.9%

Source: Bowker Annual

TABLE 5

UNIVERSITY PRESS BOOKS TREATED ON THE BLACKWELL NORTH AMERICA APPROVAL PLAN
AND AVERAGE COST, 1979-1986

	NEW	REPRINT	TOTAL	%INCREASE/ DECREASE	TOTAL COST	%INCREASE/ DECREASE	AVG.COST	PERCENT INCREASE
1979-1980	3600	146	3746		$ 81,282.87		$21.81	
1980-1981	3731	168	3899	+ 4.1%	94,701.27	+16.5%	24.58	+12.7%
1981-1982	4050	136	4186	+ 7.4%	113,072.99	+19.4%	27.19	+10.6%
1982-1983	4256	120	4376	+ 4.5%	119,923.99	+ 6.1%	27.59	+ 1.5%
1983-1984	4157	166	4323	- 1.2%	123,403.35	+ 2.9%	28.86	+ 4.6%
1984-1985	4319	176	4495	+ 4.0%	128,489.17	+ 4.1%	28.88	+.001%
1985-1986	4925	226	5151	+14.6%	152,413.97	+18.6%	30.01	+ 3.9%
TOTAL INCREASE 1979-1986	+1325	+80	+1405	+37.5%	+$ 71,131.10	+87.5%	+$ 8.20	+37.6%

56

FIGURE 1

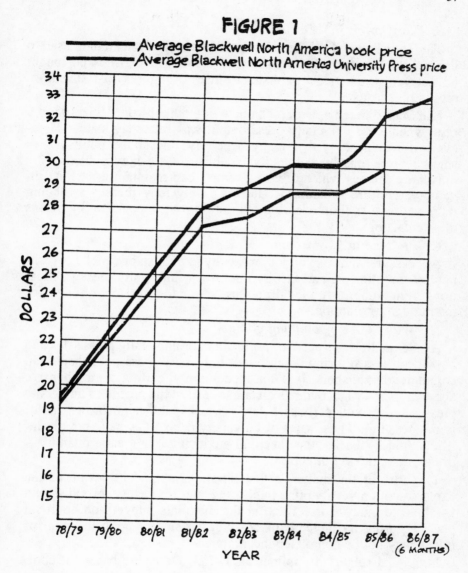

— Average Blackwell North America book price
— Average Blackwell North America University Press price

programs are called into question and budgets are reduced, many university presses are being asked to pay more of their own way. Thus, several university presses are actively pursuing profitable regional publishing programs, perhaps formerly left to a small regional private press, or are even publishing titles once construed as trade.

3. Thor Power Tool Decision.

The Thor Power Tool Decision in 1979 changed the method used to depreciate inventory. Maintenance of a strong backlist is no longer advantageous for trade publishers since strong backlist inventory means higher taxes.

Len Schrift noted a decrease in new title output from 1982-1984,[8] a time when even university press output was relatively stable. However, it would seem that many scholarly titles once published in smaller print runs by commercial publishers are now published by university presses which are tax-exempt, can maintain a backlist inventory, and are subsidized. But even university presses are being more aggressive about clearing out unsold inventory, often by means of sale catalogs.

4. The "vanity" syndrome.

As pressures increase on junior faculty to publish or perish, as competition for students and faculty intensifies, university press publications from some institutional presses offer additional opportunity for institutional promotion.

5. "We've got a good thing going."

Academic libraries account for the bulk of university press sales and have been less discriminating about university press publishers than commercial publishers. It is not uncommon in cutting comprehensive approval plans when budgets dictate to restrict the profile to university presses only (with perhaps a few sci-tech publishers thrown in for good measure). Thus, sales of university press titles have not diminished. And, if it sells, then keep on producing it in greater quantity— in this case, titles, not copies.

The crux of the matter is that librarians should be aware of the explosion of university press publishing over the past years and should continue to analyze its effect on the materials budget and approval plan. Figuring an increase of costs based simply upon inflation of prices may not be completely accurate.

Individual subject disciplines also offer interesting bases for comparison. As in the university press model, average cost per title as well as growth of an area must be considered when making a prediction for anticipated expenditures.

I have selected six subject disciplines for analysis—two from the humanities, two from the social sciences, and two from the sciences. For the humanities, art and religion were chosen. Art books have long been perceived as costly, certainly the most costly of the humanities, and they are often targets for cuts. The art book figures were derived by tabulating Fine Arts (03), Art Media (05) and Auxiliary Art (07) in the Blackwell North America statistics. Architecture (09) is excluded.

As Table 6 shows, art books have increased 37% in cost since 1979-80, but average only a minuscule 4% rise from 1980-81 to December 1986; they actually declined in price for three straight years in the early 1980s.

However, although the price per *title* of an art book has not increased radically over the past years, the number of titles treated on the approval plan has risen by 150-200 when compared with past years. Of particular note are the figures for the first half of 1986-87. It would seem as though art publishing might be dramatically increasing based on the six months' figures. But one must remember that a significant number of art books are trade—the "coffee table" type—and are published in the last half of the calendar year to appeal to the gift-giver and the Christmas market.

If we look at Figure 2, we can see graphically what has happened to the price of an art book vis-à-vis the average book cost. Indeed, in 1980-81, art books *were* expensive—some 22.6% more than the average book. But due to the decline of art book prices, that differential has totally eroded, and indeed, if the first six months of 1986-87 are any indication, the gap is widening and art books are becoming even less expensive than the average book.

What reasons could there be for this leveling off of art book pricing? Although art books are expensive to produce, improved techniques for color separation have resulted in lower costs for color reproduction.[9] Book production has sometimes relocated to lower-priced labor areas such as Hong Kong and other Asian areas from the traditional production areas of Switzerland and Italy. Finally, much of the publication of art books is trade and, although buyers do not seem to be totally resistent to higher prices, attention to maintaining a "buyable" price is probably greater than that in more technical and professional disciplines.[10]

Religion titles, however, have usually been perceived as being inexpensive, partly because of the number of devotional materials published. However, Blackwell North America has traditionally been very conservative in treating materials which could be termed as strictly devotional. Religion also has a substantial import rate, especially from the United Kingdom and India. Thus, religion books offer a basis for interesting study and comparison—perceived inexpensive prices, limited trade titles treated on the approval plan, and a fair amount of imported materials.

Table 7 shows the results of the study of religion titles gleaned by

TABLE 6

ART BOOKS TREATED ON THE BLACKWELL NORTH AMERICA APPROVAL PLAN AND AVERAGE COST, 1979-1986

	NUMBER	%INCREASE/ DECREASE	TOTAL COST	%INCREASE DECREASE	AVG. COST	%INCREASE/ DECREASE	AVERAGE BOOK COST	DIFF.
1979-1980	1001	+13.6%	$23463.88	+16.6%	$23.44	+ 2.6%	$22.37	4.8%
1980-1981	1013	+ 1.2%	31577.90	+34.6%	31.17	+33.0%	25.42	22.6%
1981-1982	939	- 7.3%	29653.76	- 6.1%	31.58	+ 1.3%	28.05	12.6%
1982-1983	918	- 2.2%	28538.72	- 3.8%	31.09	- 1.6%	29.14	6.7%
1983-1984	1040	+13.3%	31832.84	+11.5%	30.61	- 1.5%	30.13	1.6%
1984-1985	1128	+ 8.5%	34031.17	+ 6.9%	30.17	- 1.4%	30.13	.001%
1985-1986	1157	+ 2.5%	37152.31	+ 9.2%	32.11	+ 6.0%	32.43	- 1%
1986 (July/Dec)	734		23786.68		32.41	+.009%	33.19	-2.4%
TOTAL, INCREASE DECREASE 1979-1980/ 1985-1986	+156	+15.6%	+$13688.43	+58.3%	+$8.67	+37.0%		

60

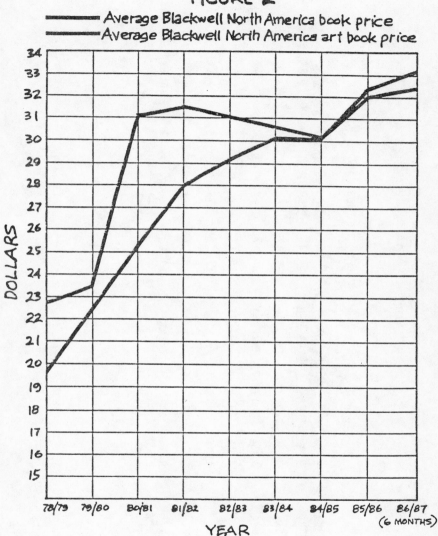

FIGURE 2

Average Blackwell North America book price
Average Blackwell North America art book price

analyzing Religion (subject descriptor 1545) in the Blackwell North America coverage and cost studies. As with university presses, it is the increased number of titles treated which causes the maximum financial impact, so that the total dollars needed to purchase the output of the Blackwell North America approval plan comprehensively in the area of religion have risen a startling 131.9% from 1979-80.

TABLE 7

RELIGION BOOKS TREATED ON THE BLACKWELL, NORTH AMERICA APPROVAL PLAN
AND AVERAGE COST, 1979-1986

	NUMBER	%INCREASE/ DECREASE	TOTAL COST	%INCREASE/ DECREASE	AVG.COST	%INCREASE/ DECREASE	AVERAGE BOOK COST	DIFFERENTIAL
1979-1980	645	+ 3.7%	$ 9734.10	+13.6%	$15.09	+ 9.5%	$22.37	- 32.5%
1980-1981	656	+ 1.7%	10409.30	+ 6.9%	15.87	+ 5.2%	25.42	-37.6%
1981-1982	845	+28.8%	13919.15	+33.7%	16.47	+ 3.8%	28.05	-41.3%
1982-1983	856	+ 1.3%	14653.92	+ 5.3%	17.12	+ 3.9%	29.14	-41.0%
1983-1984	905	+ 5.7%	17351.93	+18.4%	19.17	+12.0%	30.13	-36.4%
1984-1985	1083	+19.7%	20707.42	+19.3%	19.12	-.003%	30.13	-36.5%
1985-1986	1025	- 5.4%	22570.06	+ 9.0%	22.02	+15.2%	32.43	-32.1%
1986(July/Dec)	622		13857.67		22.28	+ 1.2%	33.19	-32.9%
TOTAL INCREASE DECREASE 1979-1980/ 1985-1986	+380	+58.9%	+$12835.96	+131.9%	+$6.93	+45.9%		

Religion titles have generally kept pace with the inflation rate of book prices overall, showing a 45.9% increase between 1979-80 and 1980-86, compared with an overall book rise of 45%. Indeed, religion books still represent good value, being some 32% cheaper than the average book, although since 1981-82, this has declined from a 41.2% differential (Figure 3). It is likely that religion titles will remain inexpensive, although perhaps not as inexpensive as previously. It would seem unlikely that publication will continue to increase at the rate it has over the past few years.

Turning now to the social sciences, two areas of particular interest — education and economics — were identified. It was my hypothesis that education titles would not have increased in cost at the rate of other subject areas due to a preponderance of textbook publishing (and concomitant treatment on the approval plan) and the number of paperbacks, spiral/ring bindings, etc., which make up education output.

Table 8 summarizes the results of the education study, using Blackwell North America figures for Education (subject description 3664) for 1979-1986.

In 1980-81 and 1981-82, the inflation rate of education books outpaced the inflation rate of books in general, as it did also in 1983-84. Thus, while education books were 32.8% less expensive than the average book in 1979-80, they are now only 27.5% less expensive, indicating that the price increases of education titles have been outstripping the average book price increase. However, the publication rate has remained relatively stable in contrast with art, religion, and university presses. Overall, education remains a subject with generally inexpensive prices (Figure 4).

On the other hand, I believed economics was probably a different story. It had been my feeling, from profiling libraries' approval plans over the years, that not only had output risen significantly but prices had too. My rationale for these hypotheses was two-fold: (1) the general public's increased interest in fiscal matters would naturally result in higher publication rates, and (2) the mathematical and statistical underpinnings of modern economics would tend to catch economics up in price to scientific and technological titles. My hypotheses proved true (Table 9) after a study of Economics (Blackwell North America thesaurus subject description 2765). As can be seen from this table, publication has jumped from 754 in 1979-80 to 1030 in 1985-86, although it is possible from preliminary figures, that publication may abate slightly this year. The differential between the average book cost and the average cost of an economics book has also declined by almost 5%. The cost of economics books for six months of 1986-87 was more

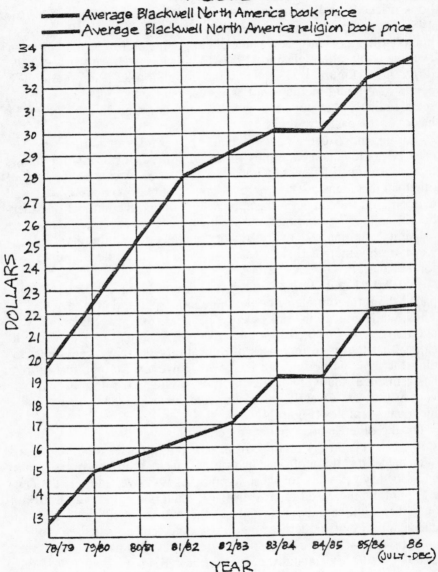

FIGURE 3

— Average Blackwell North America book price
— Average Blackwell North America religion book price

than the cost of *all* economics books for 1979-80. Clearly, economics is an area a library may wish to examine on its approval plan if its approval fund commitment is not keeping pace with overall book price and production increases. From Figure 5, we can discern that eco-

TABLE 8

EDUCATION BOOKS TREATED ON THE BLACKWELL NORTH AMERICA APPROVAL PLAN
AND AVERAGE COST, 1979-1986

	NUMBER	%INCREASE/ DECREASE	TOTAL COST	%INCREASE/ DECREASE	AVG.COST	%INCREASE/ DECREASE	AVERAGE BOOK COST	DIFFERENTIAL
1979-1980	637	+ 5.3%	$9572.80	+15.1%	$15.03	+11.9%	$22.37	-32.8%
1980-1981	733	+15.1%	12890.36	+34.7%	17.59	+17.0%	25.42	-30.8%
1981-1982	631	-13.9%	12929.30	+.003%	20.49	+16.5%	28.05	-27.0%
1982-1983	743	+17.7%	15300.82	+18.3%	20.59	+.005%	29.14	-29.3%
1983-1984	719	- 3.2%	15901.70	+ 3.9%	22.12	+ 7.4%	30.13	-26.6%
1984-1985	790	+ 9.9%	17342.50	+ 9.1%	21.95	-.008%	30.13	-27.1%
1985-1986	741	- 6.2%	17372.22	+.002%	23.44	+ 6.8%	32.43	-27.7%
1986(July/Dec)	407		9794.89		24.07	+ 2.7%	33.19	-27.5%
TOTAL INCREASE DECREASE 1979-1980/ 1985-1986	+104	+16.3%	+$7769.70	+81.5%	+$8.41	+35.9%		

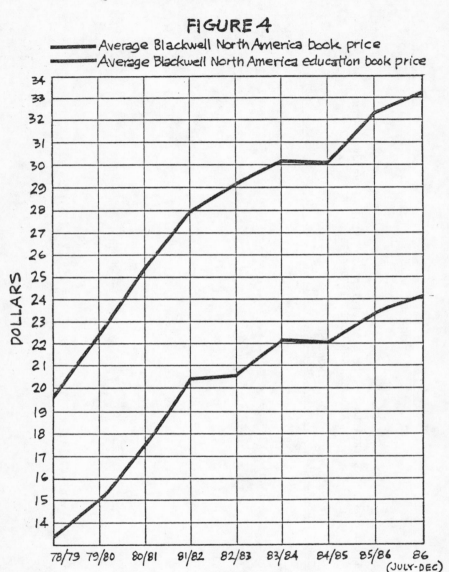

FIGURE 4

━━━ Average Blackwell North America book price
═══ Average Blackwell North America education book price

nomics has very closely followed the overall book cost increase pattern.

Moving on to the sciences, I selected earth sciences and chemistry. Geology is less reliant on the journal literature than most areas of the biological and physical sciences; monographs still assume a weighty

TABLE 9

ECONOMICS BOOKS TREATED ON THE BLACKWELL NORTH AMERICA APPROVAL PLAN
AND AVERAGE COST, 1979-1986

	NUMBER	%INCREASE/ DECREASE	TOTAL COST	%INCREASE/ DECREASE	AVG.COST	%INCREASE/ DECREASE	AVERAGE BOOK COST	DIFFERENTIAL
1979-1980	754	+16.7%	$15062.19	+39.5%	$19.98	+19.4%	$22.37	-10.1%
1980-1981	717	- 4.9%	16103.52	+ 6.9%	22.46	+12.4%	25.42	-11.6%
1981-1982	751	+ 4.7%	19880.65	+23.5%	26.41	+17.6%	28.05	- 5.6%
1982-1983	786	+ 4.7%	20841.90	+ 4.8%	26.51	+ 1.0%	29.14	- 9.0%
1983-1984	903	+14.9%	24186.80	+16.0%	26.78	+ 5.9%	30.13	-10.1%
1984-1985	943	+ 4.4%	26752.73	+10.6%	28.37	+ 6.2%	30.13	- 5.8%
1985-1986	1030	+ 9.2%	31049.28	+13.8%	30.14	+ 6.2%	32.43	- 7.1%
1986(Jul/Dec)	494		15472.74		31.32	+ 3.9%	33.19	- 5.5%
TOTAL, INCREASE DECREASE								
1979-1980/ 1985-1986	+276	+36.6%	+$15987.09	+106.0%	+$10.16	+50.9%		

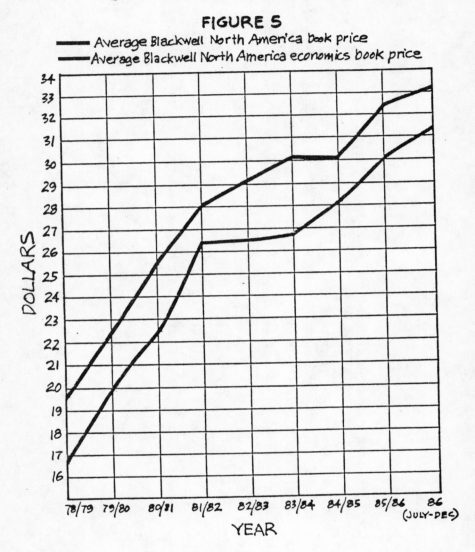

FIGURE 5
━━━ Average Blackwell North America book price
━━━ Average Blackwell North America economics book price

importance. Chemical literature, on the other hand, is more preponderant in journals.

One expects the sciences to have higher prices and greater inflation and, indeed, not even earth sciences with its monographic literature disappointed. Table 10 indicates that publications in earth sciences (51 in the Blackwell North America thesaurus) have increased but not at the rate of a subject such as religion. Likewise, although the overall funds needed have almost doubled since 1979-80, the average differ-

TABLE 10

EARTH SCIENCES BOOKS ON THE BLACKWELL NORTH AMERICA APPROVAL PLAN
AND AVERAGE COST, 1979-1986

	NUMBER	%INCREASE/ DECREASE	TOTAL COST	%INCREASE/ DECREASE	AVG.COST	%INCREASE/ DECREASE	AVERAGE BOOK COST	DIFFERENTIAL
1979-1980	185	-.005%	$ 6828.40	+34.9%	$36.91	+35.6%	$22.37	+65.0%
1980-1981	221	+19.5%	8017.95	+17.4%	36.28	- 1.7%	25.42	+42.7%
1981-1982	268	+21.3%	12055.17	+50.4%	44.98	+24.0%	28.05	+60.4%
1982-1983	263	- 1.9%	11605.15	- 3.7%	44.13	- 1.9%	29.14	+51.4%
1983-1984	300	+14.1%	13973.68	+20.4%	46.58	+ 5.6%	30.13	+54.6%
1984-1985	238	-20.7%	11667.49	-16.5%	49.02	+ 5.2%	30.13	+62.7%
1985-1986	262	+10.1%	12976.47	+11.2%	49.53	+ 1.0%	32.43	+52.7%
1986(Jul/Dec)	124		5881.32		47.43	- 4.2%	33.19	+42.9%
TOTAL INCREASE/ DECREASE								
1979-1980/ 1985-1986	+77	+41.6%	+$6148.07	+90.0%	+$12.62	+34.2%		

69

ential has held relatively constant and has recently shown signs of some decline. The price pattern is also worth noting. The astounding price increase between 1980-81 and 1981-82 has not been repeated. In fact, earth sciences tends to run, it seems, in two year spurts, and it is clear that prices have recently shown some moderation (Figure 6).

For a final subject examination, chemistry pricing (48 in the Blackwell North America hierarchical thesaurus; biochemistry [4572] is excluded) offered an interesting contrast with earth sciences. It had seemed to me that over the years chemistry book prices had escalated

FIGURE 6

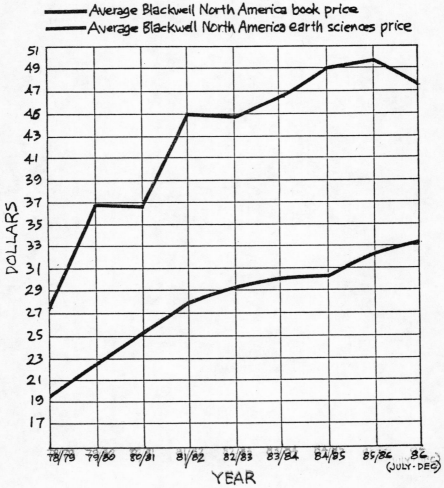

———— Average Blackwell North America book price
———— Average Blackwell North America earth sciences price

at a rate far greater than that of other disciplines, even including other disciplines in the sciences. Indeed, the jumps in chemistry prices are nothing short of astonishing with the average price of a chemistry title rising from $48.70 to $79.83 in seven years (Table 11), a pace outstripping the average book price increase by 9.3%. For libraries with approval plans, it is clear that a $75.00 — or even a $100.00 limit — is inadequate for chemistry coverage. However, it is significant that the *number* of publications has not increased at all — the increases in costs are due solely to increased price.

When compared with the average book price, we can see that the price of a chemistry book generally runs well over 100% that of an average book and rose to as much as 146% in 1985-86. However, as can be seen from Figure 7, the spread grows ever wider.

If we look at a composite graph of the Blackwell North America average book price, university press book price, and the six subject areas, some interesting observations emerge (Figure 8).

1. As has already been observed, art books are now priced more cheaply than the average book.
2. Economics books are now more expensive than the average university press book when they have been traditionally less expensive.
3. Only art has truly declined in price relative to the average book; all other subjects show a relatively concomitant increase.
4. The science subjects far surpass their counterparts, both in average price and in average price increase.
5. Religion titles have increased at a much slower rate than other areas.

Particular analysis should be made of the reasons for the significantly higher science prices. A quotation from *Alice's Adventures in Wonderland* cited in *SLJ/School Library Journal* seems to sum up science price increases vis-à-vis those in other disciplines:

> "I wish you wouldn't squeeze so" said the Dormouse, who was sitting next to her. "I can hardly breathe."
> "I can't help it," said Alice very meekly; "I'm growing."
> "You've got no right to grow *here*," said the Dormouse.
> "Don't talk nonsense," said Alice more boldly: "you know you're growing too."
> "Yes, but I grow at a reasonable pace," said the Dormouse: "not in that ridiculous fashion."[11]

TABLE 11

CHEMISTRY BOOKS TREATED ON THE BLACKWELL NORTH AMERICAN APPROVAL PLAN
AND AVERAGE COST, 1979-1986

	NUMBER	%INCREASE/DECREASE	TOTAL COST	%INCREASE/DECREASE	AVG.COST	%INCREASE/DECREASE	AVERAGE BOOK COST	DIFFERENTIAL
1979-1980	285	+ 8.8%	$13880.70	+47.0%	$48.70	+35.1%	$22.37	+117.7%
1980-1981	270	- 5.3%	13608.20	- 2.0%	50.40	+ 3.5%	25.42	+ 98.3%
1981-1982	262	- 3.0%	15678.90	+15.2%	59.84	+18.7%	28.05	+113.3%
1982-1983	266	+ 1.5%	17895.10	+14.1%	67.61	+13.0%	29.11	+132.0%
1983-1984	311	+16.9%	20430.17	+14.2%	65.69	- 3.0%	30.13	+118.0%
1984-1985	284	- 8.7%	19690.83	- 3.6%	69.33	+ 5.5%	30.13	+130.0%
1985-1986	278	- 2.1%	22193.33	+12.7%	79.83	+15.1%	32.43	+146.2%
1986(Jul/Dec)	132		9918.81		75.14	- 5.9%	33.19	+126.4%

TOTAL, INCREASE DECREASE

	NUMBER	%INCREASE/DECREASE	TOTAL COST	%INCREASE/DECREASE	AVG.COST	%INCREASE/DECREASE		
1979-1980/ 1985-1986	-8	- 2.5%	+$8312.63	+59.9%	+$26.44	+54.3%		

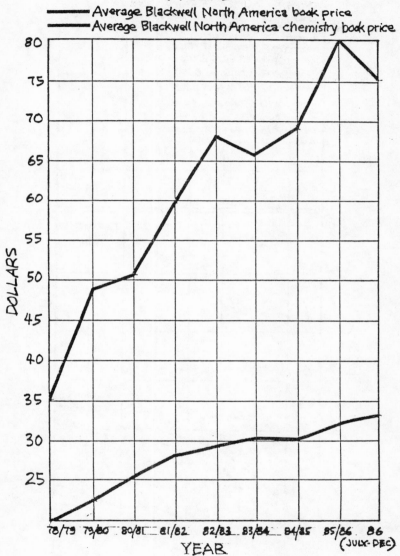

FIGURE 7

Average Blackwell North America book price
Average Blackwell North America chemistry book price

Science book prices do seem to be growing in a ridiculous fashion, but why? In an article in *Science*, as early as 1974, presently entitled "Soaring Prices and Sinking Sales of Science Monographs," Curtis G. Benjamin, former president and chairman of McGraw Hill attributed rising prices to:

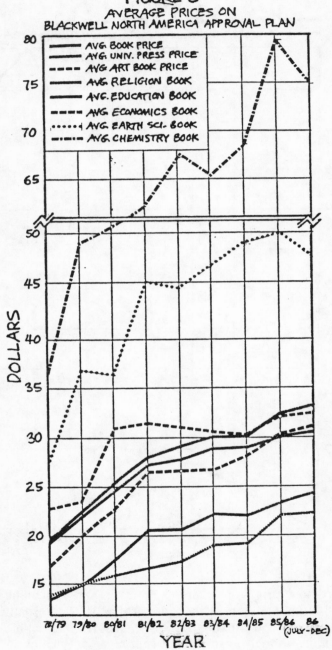

FIGURE 8
AVERAGE PRICES ON
BLACKWELL NORTH AMERICA APPROVAL PLAN

— AVG. BOOK PRICE
— AVG. UNIV. PRESS PRICE
--- AVG. ART BOOK PRICE
— AVG. RELIGION BOOK
— AVG. EDUCATION BOOK
-·- AVG. ECONOMICS BOOK
···· AVG. EARTH SCI. BOOK
—·— AVG. CHEMISTRY BOOK

DOLLARS

YEAR

78/79 79/80 80/81 81/82 82/83 83/84 84/85 85/86 86 (JULY-DEC)

1. Declining sales of monographs due to resistance of librarians to higher book prices.
2. The "twigging" phenomenon — or increasingly narrow specializations of scientists resulting in ever more limited audiences for publications.
3. Increases in photocopying and interlibrary loan. [12]

Although one may quarrel with Mr. Benjamin's observation on interlibrary loan and photocopying as a primary cause for higher prices of sci-tech books, certainly his first observations are valid as rationale for higher prices.

If it is true that higher prices mean a resultant resistance to purchase, then prices will go ever higher, for as Keith Bowker has pointed out, "Fewer sales result in smaller print runs, smaller print runs mean higher unit costs, higher unit costs mean higher prices, higher prices mean fewer sales, and so on." [13]

Publishers want to make a profit, indeed, *must* make a profit if they are to continue in business. But the costs of a book include the actual cost of production (printing, paper, binding, etc.), the publishers' overhead (marketing, warehousing, salaries, etc.); the author's royalty; and the bookseller and agents' discounts. [14] As Mr. Bowker continues to point out, booksellers want their own profits, librarians and booksellers want higher discounts, both booksellers and librarians want generous credit terms, and authors want higher royalties. Add the significant increases in overheads and production costs to fewer copies sold and it becomes apparent that prices must rise substantially. [15]

Clearly emphasis on journal publication has also had an effect on the price of a sci-tech book as libraries continue to allocate a higher percentage of their materials budgets to journals. Again, this means fewer dollars to buy monographs, resulting in unsold titles, lower profits, smaller print runs, higher unit costs, and the cycle begins again. It becomes more cost effective for publishers to put ever more of their emphasis on journals [16] where a predictable number of titles can be printed, distribution costs are low, and money is received up-front before production.

The targeted market may be another reason sci-tech publishing, in particular, is expensive. Only one-third of the sales of technical, scientific, and medical books in 1982 were to wholesalers, jobbers, or libraries whereas sales to individuals and industry accounted for almost 30%. Another 33% were to retail bookstores. [17] The fact that industrial sales are large is significant, since it is likely that a necessary book will be acquired no matter what the price, and there will be less price resistance than the stretched library or retail customer would show.

Science/technology publishing also has less competition than other types of publishing. Six science publishers (Wiley, McGraw-Hill, Academic, Prentice-Hall, Plenum and Van Nostrand) account for almost one-third of total sci-tech book revenue,[18] and only 140 companies are members of the Professional and Scholarly Division of the American Association of Publishers. It is an economic dictum that the less competition selling a product, the higher prices will be.

Additionally, sci-tech titles, by and large, have a shorter shelf-life than monographs in other fields.[20] This, coupled with the aforementioned Thor Power Tool Decision, means that it is likely that a sci-tech title, perhaps printed in a run as low as 800, will not stay in print very long. Thus, the publisher has to get the best price possible while the title is in demand. Therefore, in science and technology, there are several unique factors which, when combined, serve to drive up the price of sci-tech books faster than other subjects.

There are, however, two additional factors which should not be overlooked. One is the simple fact of profits. Judith Duke reports that sci-tech books have a higher profit than trade titles, although the data are admittedly based on a small sample. The figures she cited indicate that pretax operating income averaged 11% for sci-tech publishers and only 4.1% for trade publishers in 1982. Gross margin on sales was 60.6% for sci-tech publishers and only 43.7% for trade publishers.[21] Higher prices with their resultant higher margins, a more carefully targeted market, less likelihood of returns and remaindering, and lower discounts all contribute to higher profits.

Finally, there is the foreign phenomenon, and it is that area which offered another opportunity for interesting study. There is little data available on the cost of foreign titles distributed in the United States. Using the Blackwell North America data base as representative for foreign titles distributed in the United States and the years July 1980-June 1986, I compiled data for the most common non-North American country of origin imprints (Australia, Great Britain, India, West Germany, and the Netherlands) as well as the United States to determine what the trends in pricing were and how prices compared to the average U.S. book price. As with the subject disciplines, quantity of publication was viewed as an important adjunct factor to price.

Table 12 shows the quantity, total list price, and average list price of a U.S. book for the past six years. As can be readily seen, the average list price of a U.S. title falls approximately $3.00 below the

TABLE 12

U.S. ORIGIN BOOKS TREATED ON THE BLACKWELL NORTH AMERICA APPROVAL PLAN
AND AVERAGE COST, 1980-1986

	NUMBER	%INCREASE/ DECREASE	TOTAL COST	%INCREASE/ DECREASE	AVG.COST	%INCREASE/ DECREASE	AVERAGE BOOK COST	DIFFERENTIAL
1980-1981	15987		$349,258.03		$21.85		$25.42	-14.1%
1981-1982	16153	+ 1.0%	393,591.46	+13.6%	24.37	+11.5%	28.05	-13.2%
1982-1983	16797	+ 4.0%	435,177.88	+10.6%	25.91	+ 6.3%	29.14	-11.1%
1983-1984	18637	+11.0%	515,797.83	+18.5%	27.68	+ 6.8%	30.13	- 8.1%
1984-1985	19112	+ 2.5%	528,603.74	+ 2.5%	27.66	-.001%	30.13	- 8.2%
1985-1986	18178	- 4.9%	544,707.92	+ 3.0%	29.97	+ 8.4%	32.43	- 7.6%
TOTAL	+2191	+13.7%	+$195,449.89	+56.0%	+$8.12	+37.2%		

77

aggregate average list price. Thus, it is immediately clear that imported books carry higher prices and drive up the average list price.

As can be seen from Figure 9, the U.S. price, although lower, almost exactly parallels the pattern of the overall average price.

Australian books have proven to be less expensive than the average book, and quantity has remained relatively stable except for 1981-82 and 1982-83 (Table 13). It will be interesting to track this figure for 1986-87 and 1987-88 given the current popularity of Australian culture in the U.S. The differential between the Australian average price and the average book price has remained relatively constant, and it takes only 45.3% more dollars to purchase Australian titles in 1985-86

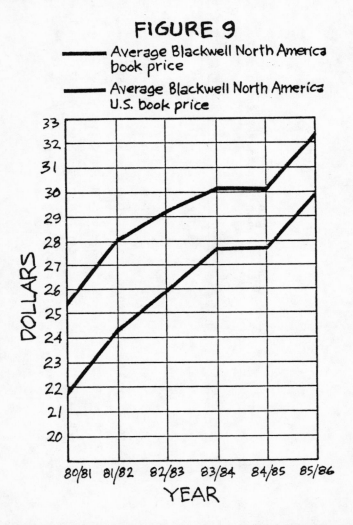

FIGURE 9

—— Average Blackwell North America book price

—— Average Blackwell North America U.S. book price

TABLE 13

AUSTRALIAN BOOKS TREATED ON THE BLACKWELL NORTH AMERICA APPROVAL PLAN AND AVERAGE COST, 1980-1986

	NUMBER	%INCREASE/ DECREASE	TOTAL COST	%INCREASE/ DECREASE	AVG.COST	%INCREASE/ DECREASE	AVERAGE BOOK COST	DIFFERENTIAL
1980-1981	169		$3818.50		$22.60		$25.42	-11.1%
1981-1982	244	+44.4%	5635.80	+47.6%	23.10	+ 2.2%	28.05	-17.6%
1982-1983	256	+ 4.9%	6256.37	+11.0%	24.44	+ 5.8%	29.14	-16.1%
1983-1984	182	-28.9%	4520.90	-27.7%	24.84	+ 1.6%	30.13	-17.6%
1984-1985	183	+.005%	5088.75	+12.6%	27.81	+12.0%	30.13	- 7.7%
1985-1986	193	+ 5.5%	5549.50	+ 9.1%	28.75	+ 3.4%	32.43	-11.3%
TOTAL	+24	+14.2%	+$1731.00	+45.3%	+6.15	+27.2%		

than it did in 1980-81, one of the lowest percentages of any subject or geographic area in my study. Figure 10 illustrates the Australian differential. One should note the 12% price jump between 1983-84 and 1984-85.

Although Australian titles held relatively steady in cost between 1980-86, the same cannot be said for Indian titles. The dollars needed to buy Indian title output on the Blackwell North America approval plan have tripled since 1980-81, both due to sharply increased prices and significantly higher output (Table 14). With a 66.8% cost increase, the price of an Indian book has gone from being 24.1% cheaper than the average book to 1% more expensive (Figure 11).

Differential pricing on journals from Great Britain and West Ger-

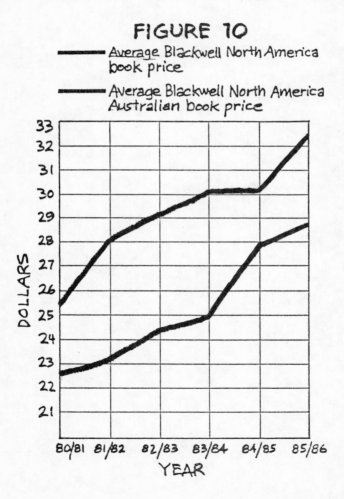

FIGURE 10

━━━━━ Average Blackwell North America book price

━━━━━ Average Blackwell North America Australian book price

TABLE 14

INDIAN BOOKS TREATED ON THE BLACKWELL NORTH AMERICA APPROVAL PLAN
AND AVERAGE COST, 1980-1986

	NUMBER	%INCREASE/ DECREASE	TOTAL COST	%INCREASE/ DECREASE	AVG. COST	%INCREASE/ DECREASE	AVERAGE BOOK COST	DIFFERENTIAL
1980-1981	247		$ 4831.95		$19.56		$25.42	-24.1%
1981-1982	288	+16.6%	6766.26	+40.0%	23.49	+20.1%	28.05	-16.3%
1982-1983	329	+14.2%	8349.90	+23.4%	25.38	+ 8.0%	29.14	-12.9%
1983-1984	488	+48.3%	12428.95	+48.9%	25.47	+.004%	30.13	-15.5%
1984-1985	509	+ 4.3%	14658.90	+17.9%	28.80	+13.1%	30.13	- 4.4%
1985-1986	454	-10.8%	14807.25	+ 1.0%	32.62	+13.3%	32.43	+ 1.0%
TOTAL	+207	+83.8%	+9975.30	+206.4%	+13.06	+66.8%		

81

FIGURE 11

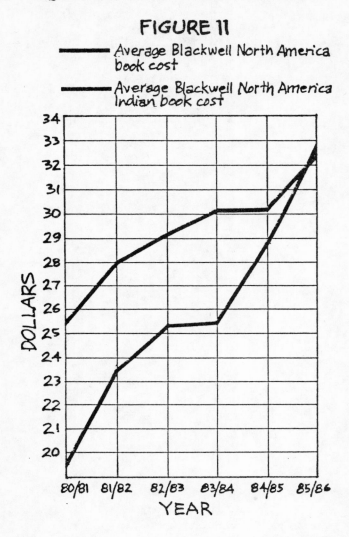

many has caused much concern among U.S. librarians. It is heartening to observe that differential pricing does not seem to be an issue when it comes to book pricing. The U.K. figures (Table 15) indicate substantially more output in 1985-86 than in 1980-81. This results not only from greater U.K. publication output within the U.K. but even more from the increasing number of British publishers locating publishing offices in the U.S., co-publishing arrangements, and rights sales.

Although publication output has increased, the average cost of a U.K. book has hardly increased at all between 1980 and 1986. Cer-

TABLE 15

BRITISH BOOKS TREATED ON THE BLACKWELL NORTH AMERICA APPROVAL PLAN
AND AVERAGE COST, 1980-1986

	NUMBER	%INCREASE/ DECREASE	TOTAL COST	%INCREASE/ DECREASE	AVG.COST	%INCREASE/ DECREASE	AVERAGE BOOK COST	DIFFERENTIAL
1980-1981	4355		$140502.28		$32.36		$25.42	+26.9%
1981-1982	5634	+29.4%	178612.37	+27.1%	31.70	- 1.7%	28.05	+13.0%
1982-1983	5874	+ 4.3%	182073.49	+ 1.9%	31.00	- 2.2%	29.14	+ 6.4%
1983-1984	6017	+ 2.4%	180664.67	-.001%	30.03	- 3.1%	30.13	- 0.3%
1984-1985	6640	+10.4%	202837.87	+12.3%	30.55	+ 1.7%	30.13	+ 1.4%
1985-1986	6113	- 7.9%	198039.31	- 2.4%	32.40	+ 6.1%	32.43	-.001%
TOTAL	1758	+40.4%	+$ 57537.03	+41.0%	+ .04	+.004%		

tainly this is a result of the strength of the dollar, since the pound was at $2.44 in 1980-81 compared to $1.44 in 1985-86. The average price of a U.K. title in England during this period rose from £14 to £21 so, in general, it can be said that the British have been quite fair in pricing their U.S. titles, although there still remains about a 15.8% price differential if books are ordered directly from England.[22] The results of a declining dollar can be seen in the latest figures, but it is particularly interesting to note that for the past three years the price of a British book has been extremely close to the price of the average book (Figure 12).

The figures are likewise heartening from West Germany (Table 16, Figure 13), although the average price is significantly higher due to

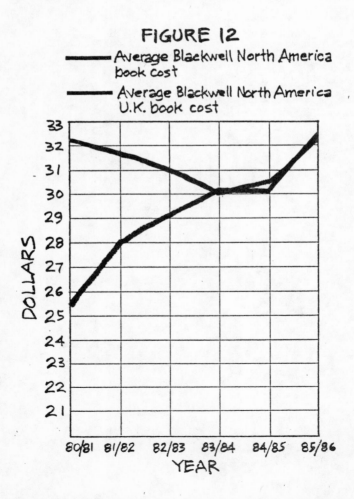

FIGURE 12
——— Average Blackwell North America book cost
——— Average Blackwell North America U.K. book cost

TABLE 16

GERMAN BOOKS ON THE BLACKWELL NORTH AMERICA APPROVAL PLAN
AND AVERAGE COST, 1980-1986

	NUMBER	%INCREASE/ DECREASE	TOTAL COST	%INCREASE/ DECREASE	AVG.COST	%INCREASE/ DECREASE	AVERAGE BOOK COST	DIFFERENTIAL
1980-1981	544		$21821.93		$40.11		$25.42	+57.8%
1981-1982	554	+ 1.8%	21754.35	-.003%	39.27	- 2.1%	28.05	+40.0%
1982-1983	742	+33.9%	27558.95	+26.7%	37.14	- 5.4%	29.14	+27.5%
1983-1984	758	+ 2.2%	27948.20	+ 1.4%	36.87	-.007%	30.13	+22.4%
1984-1985	689	- 9.1%	27846.55	-.004%	40.42	+ 9.6%	30.13	+34.2%
1985-1986	719	- 4.4%	33242.40	+19.4%	46.23	+14.4%	32.43	+42.6%
TOTAL	+175	+32.2%	+$11420.47	+52.3%	+$ 6.12	+15.3%		

FIGURE 13

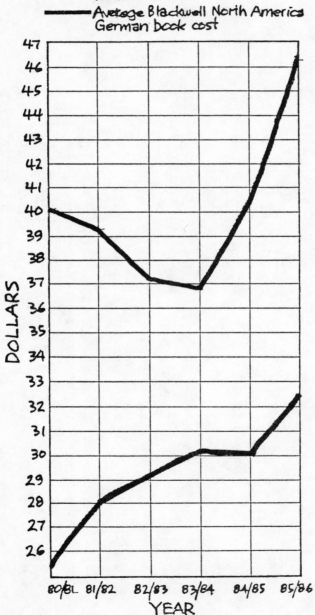

─── Average Blackwell North America book cost

─── Average Blackwell North America German book cost

the proportion of sci-tech materials imported into the U.S. Nonetheless, prices declined for four straight years. Output has risen significantly, although the last two years have shown a decline. There may be some cause for concern if the increases in average price for 1984-85 and 1985-86 continue for 1986-87, although this jump can be attributed to the decline of the dollar and the overall strength of the deutschmark. Still the overall differential has declined more than 15%, so that while German books may still not be in line with other countries, they have, it seems, generally been priced fairly.

Finally, we come to the Netherlands (Figure 14). Table 17 tells a very different story from that of the U.K. and West Germany. In just six short years, the total dollar value of Dutch books has almost doubled, due not only to a rise in publication but also a corresponding rise in prices. Indeed, from 1980-81 through 1983-84, a time when both the German and British prices declined each year, the Dutch prices rose, although they did dip in 1984-85.

According to an article appearing in the August 15, 1986, *Publishers' Weekly*, sci-tech publishing is the most successful and profitable arm of the Dutch publishing industry with an export business of almost $200 million yearly in books and journals, which is increasing about 10-15% each year.[23] Of the 800 new book titles published each year, the Elsevier group publishes approximately 500 titles, the Kluwer group about 350.[24]

Are Dutch publications expensive because they are sci-tech oriented? Or are sci-tech publications expensive because of the dominance of Dutch publications? I will not attempt to draw conclusions here because further research is needed in regard to price differentials if Dutch titles are purchased abroad. However, in fairness, the average cost has not increased excessively except for 1981-82, in general a period of high inflation, and price differential has actually declined.

Figure 15 summarizes prices of foreign titles distributed in the U.S. The composite graph reveals that prices in 1980-81 were much further apart from the average book for all countries studied except for Germany and the Netherlands. It is interesting to note that price differentials by country have narrowed over the past five years.

Although much work remains to be done in analysis of both publication rate increases and average costs by subject and country of origin, some conclusions can be drawn from this limited study.

First, when considering approval cuts, libraries may wish to look at country of origin as a method of retrenchment. However, it is one thing to cut Australia, with a total dollar volume of $4000, but quite another to cut the Netherlands, with a total volume of $60,000.

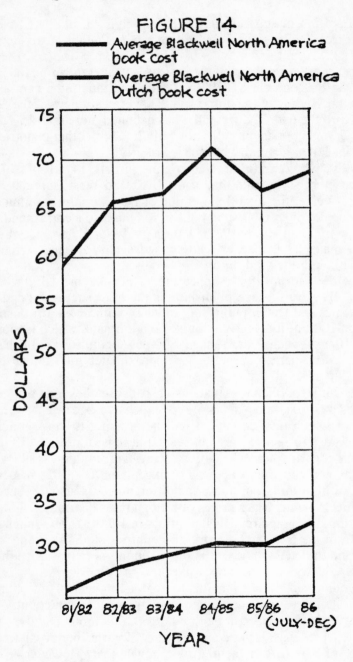

FIGURE 14

━━━ Average Blackwell North America
        book cost

━━━ Average Blackwell North America
        Dutch book cost

TABLE 17

DUTCH BOOKS TREATED ON THE BLACKWELL NORTH AMERICA APPROVAL PLAN
AND AVERAGE COST, 1980-1986

	NUMBER	%INCREASE/DECREASE	TOTAL COST	%INCREASE/DECREASE	AVG.COST	%INCREASE/DECREASE	AVERAGE BOOK COST	DIFFERENTIAL
1980-1981	517		$30578.89		$59.15		$25.42	+132.7%
1981-1982	689	+33.3%	45251.65	+48.0%	65.68	+11.0%	28.05	+134.2%
1982-1983	833	+20.9%	55270.80	+22.1%	66.35	+ 1.0%	29.14	+127.7%
1983-1984	800	- 4.0%	56835.00	+ 2.8%	71.04	+ 7.1%	30.13	+135.8%
1984-1985	818	+ 2.3%	54502.55	- 4.1%	66.63	- 6.2%	30.13	+121.1%
1985-1986	863	+5.5%	59290.05	+ 8.8%	68.70	+ 3.1%	32.43	+111.8%
TOTAL	+346	+66.9%	+$28711.16	+93.9%	+$ 9.55	+16.1%		

FIGURE 15

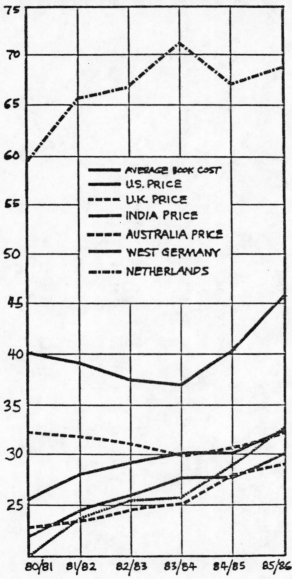

U.S. AND FOREIGN BOOK COST
BLACKWELL NORTH AMERICA APPROVAL PLAN

Second, if a library is faced with cutting approval plan titles, it should look at publication rates by discipline. Some subjects will need tighter pruning than others if publication rates have escalated. Costs per discipline should also be examined.

Third, librarians should realize that booksellers face considerable pressure from rising prices which have ramifications for the business. Booksellers too face the prospect of lower unit sales but have fixed operating costs in physical plant, computers, and labor. Is it any wonder that book vendors all want to sell university press approval plans (with vastly increased publication) or Dutch publications or sci-tech approval plans? A core list of sci-tech publishers is quite attractive for book vendors — high gross margins can make up for some lost unit sales and higher discounts.

Fourth, libraries should analyze approval budgets to determine if their approval budget increases have kept pace not only with inflation but also publication rates. Clearly, most libraries have not kept pace with either. A simple prediction of inflation will not accurately forecast expenditures; publication rate inflation must also be factored into the projection. Finally, approval plans are still the most cost-effective means of acquiring books. A fascinating price study awaits the individual who investigates price increases of individual titles one year later, especially on sci-tech books. Approval plans still bring in the title, however, priced at first price. Thus, they remain the best protection against inflation and offer librarians an excellent means of budget control.

NOTES

1. Carolyn J. Mooney, "Bad News for Public Colleges: Economies Slump in Many States," *The Chronicle of Higher Education*, 18 February 1987, 1.

2. "AFSCME Strike Closes Free Library of Philadelphia; Dallas and Houston Cut Pay," *American Libraries* 17 (1986): 505.

3. "Budget Squeeze to Cut Acquisitions at UT-Austin," *Library Hotline*, 1 December 1986, 2.

4. John F. Baker, "1986: Looking Back," *Publisher's Weekly*, 9 January 1987, 35.

5. *The Bowker Annual of Library and Book Trade Information*, 30th ed., ed. and comp. by Julia Moore (New York: Bowker, 1985): 440-1 and *The Bowker Annual of Library and Book Trade Information*, 29th ed., ed. and comp. by Julia Moore (New York: Bowker, 1984): 387-8.

6. Herbert S. White, "Library Materials Prices and Academic Library Practice: Between Scylla and Charybdis," *The Journal of Academic Librarianship* 5 (March 1979): 21.

7. Frederick C. Lynden, "Library Materials Cost Studies," *Library Resources and Technical Services* 27 (April 1983): 156-7.

8. Leonard Schrift, "After Thor, What's Next?" *Library Acquisitions: Practice and Theory* 9, no. 1 (1985): 61.

9. John Nicoll, "The Economics of Book Publishing," *Art Libraries Journal* 3 (Winter 1978): 21-2.

10. See Leonard A. Wood, "Buyers Not Fighting Higher Prices," *Publisher's Weekly*, 11 April 1986, 24; idem, "Buyers Expect to Pay More for Nonfiction," *Publishers' Weekly*, 30 March 1984, 22; and idem, "What Customers Expect to Pay for Their Books," *Publishers' Weekly*, 3 June 1983, 48, for results of The Gallup Survey on book pricing.

11. Lewis Carroll, *Alice's Adventures in Wonderland*, cited in "The Plain Truth About Book Dollars," *SLJ/School Library Journal* 32 (March 1986): 81.

12. Curtis A. Benjamin, "Soaring Prices and Sinking Sales of Science Monographs," *Science*, 25 January 1974, 282-3.

13. Keith Bowker, "Are Books Expensive?" *Chemistry and Industry*, 2 April 1977, 167.

14. Ibid.

15. Ibid.

16. Alexander Hellemans, "Monographs in Decline," *Publishers' Weekly*, 15 August 1986, 22.

17. Judith A. Duke, *The Technical, Scientific and Medical Publishing Market* (White Plains, N.Y.: Knowledge Industry Publications, 1985): 41.

18. Ibid., 34.

19. Ibid., 33.

20. Hellemans, "Monographs in Decline," 22.

21. Duke, 54.

22. Gerald Pridmore, "The Pricing of UK Books in the United States." (B.H. Blackwell, Oxford, England, 27 November 1986, Mimeographed), 3.

23. Alexander Hellemans, "Science Publishing: At Home in Holland," *Publishers' Weekly*, 15 August 1986, 24.

24. Ibid., 26-8.

Projecting Materials Costs:
Basis for Effective Decision Making

Edna Laughrey

INTRODUCTION

In the 1970s librarians were well-prepared with sound documentation to go to their funding sources, hat in hand, begging for more and more dollars to keep abreast of ever-creeping inflation. By the early 1980s they had a difficult time requesting more funds to cover inflation because common wisdom was that inflation had waned. What then could they do to get more money when it was obvious that a static book budget would not buy as much as it had in previous years? What was causing a loss of purchasing power? How could they prove the loss of purchasing power?

Librarians are once again in the position of losing buying power and we have not kept current on monitoring the elements that impact our budgets. We must identify the factors that affect our purchasing power, develop means to measure their influence and prepare reports that address our local institutions.

FACTORS AFFECTING THE COST OF MATERIALS

A variety of factors affect the cost of materials. The most obvious of these are economic factors that are beyond the control of libraries, publishers, and vendors; namely, inflation and fluctuations in exchange rates. Other examples of uncontrollable factors that influence the cost of materials include court rulings on the tax liability of inventories and trade policies that result in import/export restrictions. It is important to look at these factors, even though there is usually very little we can do to manipulate them, because they are the stimuli that prompt internal changes in the way publishers and vendors do business with each other and with libraries.

Edna Laughrey is Head of Acquisitions at the University of Michigan.

External Factors

What do we know about inflation? We know it has dramatically affected our purchasing power, but we can no longer point to a galloping overall inflation rate to ask for funding increases. The U.S. inflation rate has been relatively low for the past several years. Prices for domestic periodicals, however, have increased at a rate significantly above the U.S. inflation rate. Current estimates are that the periodical costs will increase between 15-20% for 1987 for research libraries while the monographic rate will increase less than 10%.

If the U.S. inflation rate is the standard against which increases in the cost of domestic periodicals are compared, then fluctuations in the exchange rate of the U.S. dollar against foreign currencies are the means by which we determine increases or decreases in the cost of foreign materials. The change in the costs of foreign materials from one year to the next should reflect the change in the exchange rate plus the domestic inflation in the country of origin. The stronger the dollar is against a particular foreign currency, the more materials we can buy for our dollars; the weaker the dollar, the fewer materials we can buy. In point of fact, prices have ranged back and forth for a few years as the value of the dollar against foreign currencies has continued to shift. One point to consider is that although American libraries have been losing buying power as the strength of the dollar weakens, the same was true for European libraries when their currencies were weak. Last year's decline in the average price for British books was attributed in part to the weakened dollar.[1] The international rate of exchange has been influenced significantly by U.S. trade policy. Current U.S. policy would appear to be one of keeping the dollar weak with the expectation that a weak dollar is good for the U.S. balance of trade. Foreign businesses are more likely to invest in the American market during periods when the dollar is weak.

Between January 1985 and December 1986 the dollar weakened appreciably against the currencies of some of our most active trading partners. During this time the West German mark increased in value by 60.2% and the Japanese yen by 55%. A more current look at the increases proves that we are continuing to lose purchasing power in foreign markets. In February 1987 the mark increased 9.25% and the yen 4.8% over the January exchange rate.

In early 1987, Lawrence Knause, international economist at the University of California, San Diego, predicted that "the dollar will probably go down another 20% over time against the currencies of the major industrial countries."[2] The dollar was expected to continue to decline "until it reaches a level where it might produce the results Washington wants."[3]

In addition to devaluing the dollar, the federal government has attempted to protect certain domestic industries from foreign competition by establishing import restrictions for some foreign products. These restrictions can have adverse effects on the export activities of American publishers. Last year, the federal government imposed a five-year tariff on Canadian cedar shingles and the Canadian government retaliated by imposing a 10% surcharge on certain American books and periodicals imported into the country.[4] Even though Canadian libraries could be expected to suffer most from this decision, it would be reasonable to expect American publishers to pass on their losses to domestic consumers in the form of higher costs.

Yet another example of an external factor impacting the publishing industry was the U.S. Supreme Court's 1979 ruling that Thor Power Tool Company could not reduce the valuation of warehouse stock for tax reasons unless the stock was disposed of or sold for reduced prices.[5] A year after the ruling, librarians and publishers alike were distressed to read that the Internal Revenue Service, in response to the Supreme Court's decision against Thor Power Tool, had ruled that publishers could no longer discount the value of unsold materials and that full value must be declared for tax purposes.[6] This ruling prompted dramatic changes in publishing practices, changes that have adversely affected the price of books. Print-runs have been smaller and consequently materials have been going out of print at a more rapid rate. Since economies of scale have been reduced, costs have gone up. Publishers have tended to produce smaller first printings and to evaluate seriously the need for a second printing. There continues to be some unproven concern that slow-selling, scholarly works will not be published because no publisher is willing to take the risk.

The publishing industry has had some positive advancements that were stimulated by the Thor Tool decision, including new or enhanced programs offering on-demand publishing and increased prevalence of publishers establishing programs for small print runs of certain materials. But, once again, these were changes prompted by external factors.

Internal Factors

Inflation, fluctuations in the exchange rate, changes in tax regulations, foreign trade policy and protectionist measures all have an influence on publishing, both foreign and domestic, and are reflected in policies, procedures, and practices of publishers, vendors, and libraries. There is a wide array of factors within the publishing industry that have molded the policies that affect the cost of materials that libraries purchase.

Differential Pricing

The effects of differential pricing on U.S. libraries have been well-documented. As Marcia Tuttle pointed out at the Charleston Conference in 1985, British publishers in 1976 began selling their periodicals with a new North American price quoted in U.S. dollars, when the dollar began falling substantially against European currencies. This new price was higher than the "overseas" price charged to countries outside of North America and Britain, and higher still than the domestic price charged to U.K. subscribers. The North American prices continued to be quoted in dollars, even when the dollar began rising rapidly again in the early 1980s.[7]

What resulted was a wide difference in the price of British journals charged to U.K. and North American subscribers. British publishers later indicated they were rather amazed that North American libraries tolerated this practice for several years without protest, but they continued nonetheless to raise the North American price. It was not until about 1984 that American libraries began to realize that their stronger dollars were not buying additional British materials, as was the case with materials from other foreign countries against whose currency the dollar was doing well.[8]

The ensuing complaints resulted in pressure being applied against the British publishers to eliminate or greatly reduce the price differentials. British publishers to some extent have been responsive to this pressure. As Charles Hamaker reported at the 1987 ALA Midwinter Meeting in Chicago, the average difference in the journal prices charged for North American and U.K. libraries has been cut nearly in half, from an average of 67% more for North American libraries in 1984. Even so, Hamaker noted that the British have been closing the gap by raising prices for their U.K. subscribers. North American libraries have benefitted only in that outrageous differentials seem to be on the wane, while outrageous prices remain.

Publisher/Vendor Relationships

Academic libraries find it convenient and beneficial to employ vendors and subscription agents for acquiring monographs and serials. Changes in the services by both publishers and vendors will inevitably have an impact on the costs associated with acquiring library materials.

Some British publishers worked very hard to prevent the practice of "buying round" once it became obvious that American libraries were asking their foreign subscription agents to acquire British periodicals at the vastly cheaper U.K. rate. The publishers claimed this practice was unfair.

Some publishers base a "decision on whether or not to sell to a purchaser . . . upon the location of the invoicing address rather than the actual shipment address"; others "make the decision as to whether or not to sell a journal from their home office based upon the location of the shipping address of the journal."[10] What we have is a situation in which some publishers will not sell to vendors and some publishers will not sell directly to overseas libraries.

In the last couple of years we have encountered several examples of publishers eliminating the discount to vendors and consequently vendors needing to add handling charges or refusing to sell the publications from the company. This practice translates into higher costs being passed along to libraries that use vendors.[11]

In addition, some publishers "demand to know ultimate destination of journals purchased through subscription agent"; the publisher is asking the vendor to inform them of all customers who are to receive the materials of that publisher.[12] In 1986 VCH began to require that all subscriptions for North American customers be purchased from their North American branch office in Deerfield Beach, Fla., at the inflated U.S. distribution price.[13] Bowker in 1986 decided that it would no longer sell some 30 or 40 of its most popular titles (e.g., *Books in Print*) through vendors.[14]

Licensing Fees

Gordon and Breach Science Publishers in 1986 attempted to impose a fee of 10% on the 1987 renewal price of each of its titles for a "License to Photocopy." Libraries were offered the alternative of signing an agreement not to permit photocopying of the Gordon and Breach titles.[15]

Foreign Currency

Some publishers have changed the country in which they will post their prices and have selected countries where they feel they will get the most stable currency and value for their money. The implications and ramifications of this change are not yet known.

Foreign Buyouts

The weakened U.S. dollar makes it easier for foreign businesses to invest in the American market. In 1986, foreign publishers began a more active campaign of buying up American publishing houses. There have been a number of reasons advanced for these acquisitions, ranging from the declining birthrate on the European side of the Atlantic to the perceived safety of the U.S. as an investment haven. What the long term effects of these buyouts will be remains to be seen. It may be a "breath of fresh air," or it may be that European and Japanese owners intend to use their American profits to subsidize publishing activities at home.[16]

Publishing Output

The more publishers produce, the more libraries are pressured to buy what has been published. Research libraries, especially, are determined to acquire as much of the total scholarly output as possible. One problem is that the output shows no signs of abating despite our concerns about the Thor Tool impact. In fact, British publishers' output increased again in 1986, with a 7% increase in new titles and 16.5% increase in reprints over 1985.[17] Overall, British publishing output has tripled in the past 30 years and doubled in the past 20 years. If we are to acquire those additional materials, we must have more money to spend.

PUBLISHED SOURCES ON MATERIALS COSTS

The R.R. Bowker Company compiles information on the production and pricing of books. This information appears twice a year in Bowker's *Publisher's Weekly*, first in the spring in preliminary form and then again in the fall when the final figures are compiled. The data are also presented, along with information on foreign monographic materials and foreign and domestic serials, each year in the fall edition of *The Bowker Annual*.

The Bowker reports include data on the production of American hardbound and trade paperback books, mass market paperback titles, paperbacks other than mass market, imported hardbound and trade paperback books, and translations into English. In addition, the report provides data on average per volume prices for hardbound books (including a breakdown for hardcovers costing less than $81), mass market paperbacks, and trade paperbacks. Based on the formal bibliographical listings in Bowker's *Weekly Record/American Book Publishing Record* database, this information is presented for 23 subject categories (based on Dewey Decimal Classifications) ranging from agriculture, art and biography to sports, recreation, technology and travel.[18]

The Bowker Annual also includes data on foreign published materials. Pricing information for British academic books is obtained from the publications of the Centre for Library and Information Management (CLAIM) of Loughbrough University of Technology. Presented according to broad Dewey classes, the data include number of books published per year and average price in British pounds. The 1985 *Bowker Annual* report noted that "these data, the only available for British books, should be used with caution." It cited a survey indicating a high incidence of pre-1982 imprints and academic titles without prices in the 1983 *British National Bibliography*, the basis of the CLAIM pricing study.[19] German book prices are compiled from the *Buch und Buchhandel in Zahlen*, with three separate tables for (1) all German books, (2) German paperback books, and (3) German hardcover and scholarly paperback books. Also reported are the Latin American acquisitions of eight major U.S. research libraries, including numbers of copies and average cost per copy purchased. The figures are compiled by the SALALM (Seminars on the Acquisition of Latin American Library Materials) Acquisitions Committee.

Production of the U.S. Periodicals Price Index was taken over by the Faxon Company in 1984 at the request of and with cooperation of the American Library Association's Resources and Technical Services Division Library Materials Price Index Committee. The report looks at price data for more than 3,600 titles in Faxon's online files, producing average subscription rates for 24 subject categories ranging from agriculture, business and economics to zoology.[20] One advantage of Faxon's producing the index is that it is current to a relatively high degree; the most recent price information for the vast majority of the titles is supplied to Faxon directly by the publishers, and price information for titles not supplied through Faxon is obtained from publishers over the telephone.[21]

In addition to the U.S. Periodicals Price Index, Faxon's Rebecca T. Lenzini also annually compiles comparative three-year price reviews for domestic and foreign serial titles. The most recent of these appeared in the September 1986 *The Serials Librarian*. The report includes price analyses of titles in the Faxon Title File and titles that are indexed in selected abstracting and indexing sources; average prices paid by type of institution; average prices paid based on number of titles invoiced per type of institution; one-year change in average price for foreign and domestic titles.[22]

Unfortunately, there are drawbacks to these sources, the most obvious being that they are retrospective in nature; they tell us where we have been, not necessarily where we are going. The Faxon periodical prices update is probably the most current of these tools, but even so the information contained therein relates to the previous fiscal year. By the time the update appeared in September 1986 predicting "1987 foreign journal prices which are even higher than those experienced this year," libraries had already received invoices reflecting those higher prices.[23] Likewise, price information for foreign materials tends to be a minimum of 18 months old by the time it appears in *The Bowker Annual*, and information on domestic book production and prices is for the previous fiscal year.

Another drawback to relying on these sources is that they do not always provide information in the detail an individual library desires. It is nice to know that average foreign price of Faxon periodical titles "increased 22% over 1985, from $81.77 to $99.76 in 1986."[24] This service will be more valuable when they are able to provide a breakdown by individual foreign countries.

According to Dora Biblarz, a final drawback to the price indexes is that

> they do not address the needs of academic libraries since they include many popular books, self-help titles and other materials these libraries do not generally collect . . . data do not include books published by non-trade publishers or in esoteric, highly specialized subjects.[25]

In the meantime, individual libraries are left with the need to determine to what extent costs are rising and in what areas. Librarians can and do compile their own information in attempting to predict changes in materials costs. In reporting on the periodicals price index developed at Widener Library, Clack and Williams emphasized that the key is for "a library that does not already have average price information (to) compile it for a period of time," specifically nine years.[26]

LIBRARY SPECIFIC STUDIES

The staff of the University of Michigan Library has been examining the prices of monographs and serials to determine the patterns of price changes and then to identify the factors that affect changes in prices of materials. Since specific pricing data had not been collected in an ongoing fashion before we began this process, the trick has been to ferret out and make sense of the existing data. To accomplish this task, we have taken something of the post-hole approach, digging here and there as deeply as we can, relying heavily on existing information in our automated acquisitions system. We seem to have many more questions than answers. The results of these studies are discussed below.

Monographic Expenditures

Using our automated acquisitions system, we examined three elements of monographic expenditures:

Average Amount Encumbered

Have we been accurately encumbering prices for foreign materials? Are the differences between what was encumbered and what was paid accounted for by changes in the exchange rate or have additional charges been included? How do we keep encumbrances accurate and up to date when the exchange rate varies so quickly?

To look at the average amount encumbered for foreign monographic titles versus the average amount actually paid, we ran a boolean search of our automated acquisitions system database to find all paid records (including firm orders, approval plan books, and approval plan form selections) for British, Dutch, German, Spanish, French and Italian materials. We eliminated all records for materials that had estimated encumbered prices. Because the system database is routinely purged of materials which have been paid for and cataloged, the items found represent only items that had not been cataloged; consequently, the boolean search found relatively few records for 1982/1983 (the first records entered into Michigan's database) and many more records for 1985/86.

For each country, the total amount encumbered and the total amount paid for each year were divided by the number of titles to arrive at an average encumbered price and an average paid price. The two averages were then compared to determine whether the actual paid amount was above or below the price encumbered. The results varied widely from year to year and country to country, as indicated in the chart below:

PERCENTAGE DIFFERENCE
AMOUNT PAID VS. AMOUNT ENCUMBERED

Country	82/83	83/84	84/85	85/86	Overall
Britain	+30.0	- 9.4	+ 5.3	+ 0.2	+ 3.5
Netherlands		+ 8.2	+24.7	+12.9	+ 9.4
Germany	- 0.3	+ 1.1	-13.1	-16.8	-12.7
Spain		+56.8	+45.5	+84.2	+64.1
France	- 8.2	+ 4.0	+11.4	+19.3	+10.1
Italy		+10.4	- 5.9	+31.1	+27.7

For example, the average amount paid for British materials each year ranged from 9.39% below to 30% above the amount encumbered, with only a 0.17% difference for the latest year. Likewise, Italian materials saw average paid amounts ranging from 5.9% below to 31% above the average encumbered price and French materials ranged from 8.2% below to 19% above.[27]

The average amount paid for Dutch materials was consistently above the amount encumbered, ranging from 8.23% to 24.74% above; however, the difference was not as markedly large as the Spanish materials, for which the average paid amount ranged from 45.5% to 84.1% above what was encumbered.[28] By contrast, the average amount paid for German materials was less than the amount encumbered (ranging 0.3% to 16% below) except for one year (1.1% above).

There did not appear to be any correlation between these figures and changes in the exchange rate of the dollar against the relevant foreign currencies. Given that Acquisitions routinely orders materials without having complete pricing information and oftentimes must guess at prices, the lack of an overall well-defined pattern was not too surprising. Nonetheless, it did appear that we were consistently overencumbering slightly for German materials and markedly underencumbering for Spanish materials.

The latter case prompted us to look more closely at our orders for Spanish materials. We discovered that our Spanish dealer had been supplying us with price information in dollars rather than pesetas without indicating the date at which the price was posted. Consequently, we did not know at the time of inputting whether the dollar price was still consistent with the exchange rate for pesetas that the vendor had used.

Postal Charges

In cases where there was a significant difference between what we encumbered for a title and what we paid the vendor, we checked to see how much of the difference could be accounted for by postage and handling charges. Also, as a result of the sharp difference between the encumbered and actual paid amount for Spanish materials, we checked our Spanish invoices to find that there were hefty charges for shipping and handling. These charges seemed to account for most of the difference between the encumbered and actual paid amounts for the Spanish materials. We also checked our Dutch invoices to find that postage and handling charges had been added, again accounting in part for the difference between the encumbered and actual paid amounts. Another consideration was the discovery of one Dutch title available through a Dutch source that added postage and handling charges and a British source without the added postage and handling charges, a substantial savings.

Exchange Rate Changes and Encumbrances

Given the change in the exchange rate, what would we be paying for these materials now as opposed to the time at which they were encumbered? We wanted to know what impact the change in foreign currencies against the dollar would have on our outstanding orders. Encumbrances are valuable working numbers as they tell us how much we have in outstanding orders and they are needed to prevent us from over or under-expanding our budgets. Rapidly changing exchange rates adversely affect this management device because our encumbrance systems do not record orders in foreign currency and then re-convert the encumbrance on a daily basis at the new exchange rate.

At the University of Michigan we performed a study to see how much our encumbrances were affected by the change in exchange rate and the delay between the ordering and receiving material. In October 1986 we ran a boolean search on our automated acquisitions system and gathered all the unfilled orders that had been placed with our major foreign vendors between January and June of 1986. We asked the system to total the amount encumbered each month for each vendor. The next step was to convert the encumbered amount back to the original foreign currency at the rate for the day it was ordered. We then reconverted that foreign currency amount back to U.S. dollars at the rate of exchange for the end of October. The following chart shows the percent difference between the original encumbered amount and the price we would have paid had the material arrived and been paid for in late October 1986.

IMPACT OF CHANGE IN EXCHANGE RATE ON AMOUNTS ENCUMBERED FOR FOREIGN MATERIALS

Country	1/86	2/86	3/86	4/86	5/86	6/86	OVERALL
Britain	1.07	1.40	-1.21	-5.25	-5.90	-4.02	-1.75
France	13.12	10.39	3.35	8.56	4.14	11.60	7.48
Italy	21.60	17.30	8.19	12.30	9.20	10.70	9.56
Netherlands	20.49	17.96	10.13	14.59	6.72	14.17	13.92
Germany	24.90	19.80	10.25	13.10	7.28	12.20	12.44

Using Approval Plan Vendor Management Reports

The University of Michigan Library has a large number of approval/blanket order plans. To allow for the receipt of duplicate material in collections that overlap in scope, we chose to have individual plans profiled for each of our divisional libraries. As a consequence we have over twenty profiles with eight vendors. The profiles are uniquely defined by subject, publisher and/or country of publication.

During 1985/86, the University of Michigan Library purchased 10,388 titles on six of our approval plans. This figure represents a 2.8% increase over 10,104 titles purchased on the same six plans during 1984/85. By contrast, overall expenditures for 1985/86 for the approval plans were $345,475, a 17.2% increase over 1984/85 expenditures of $294,725.

The average price per book increased from $29.17 in 1984/85 to $33.26 in 1985/86, a 14% increase. For 1985/86, the average price per book per approval plan ranged from $16.71 to $53.08. Britain had the largest change in the average price per book for 1985/86, an increase of 38.9% over 1984/85. The following chart gives the comparative data on seven plans with the six vendors.

APPROVAL PLAN COMPARISON 1984/85 TO 1985/86

Vendor	Titles Purchased		Amount Expended		Average Price Per Book		
	84/85	85/86	84/85	85/86	84/85	85/86	% Change
US1	1707	2048	$ 73,244	$ 92,312	$42.91	$45.07	+ 5.0
Britain	2002	2240	$ 42,896	$ 66,674	$21.42	$29.76	+ 38.9
US2	3035	2858	$ 88,456	$ 89,257	$29.14	$31.23	+ 7.2
US3	2394	2273	$ 56,858	$ 58,856	$23.75	$25.89	+ 9.0
Germany	454	359	$ 6,370	$ 5,999	$14.03	$16.71	+ 17.2
US4	512	610	$ 26,901	$ 32,377	$52.54	$53.08	+ 1.0
Totals	10104	10388	$294,725	$345,475	$29.17	$33.26	+ 14.0

Most of the data included in this chart was supplied on management reports provided by the vendor. We were fascinated by the shift in the number of volumes acquired versus the amount spent. From US1 we received 20% more material and spent 26% more. When we looked at Britain the story was more dramatic, volumes increased by 11.9% and costs by 55.4%.

We had some difficulty believing these data were correct and decided to do some studies with the information we had available locally. We performed studies of approval plan books to attempt to verify the vendor supplied data and determine whether we were paying more for materials this year than last year. Logic would tell us that we have been paying more. Certainly we must be expending more for foreign items since the exchange rate has not been in our favor for most currencies.

Materials in our automated acquisitions system are eligible to be purged from that system after they have been received and cataloged for six weeks. Consequently, our data were limited in quantity, but we felt the sample size was sufficiently large to make the trend results reliable. Our study involved collecting paid amounts and number of copies acquired data according to the month in which the item was paid. We then planned to compare the average cost per item data from one month to the next. We further divided the study by vendor so we could determine the differences in costs for various foreign countries and among our domestic vendors, just as our vendors had done with the data they supplied.

APPROVAL PLAN BOOKS/AVERAGE PRICE PER COPY BY PLAN

Country	Jul-Dec 1985	Jan-Jul 1986	Jul-Dec 1986	Ave.Price % Incr.	Ave.Price % Incr. Jul-Jun	Overall % Incr. Jul-Jun
Britain	19.06	24.29	29.66	27.44	22.11	55.61
Germany	NA	16.81	19.54	NA	16.24	16.24
Spain	9.43	11.24	13.98	19.19	24.38	48.25
US5	22.48	27.81	26.72	23.71	-3.92	18.86
US6	19.33	20.72	25.37	7.19	22.44	31.25
US7	NA	44.81	47.20	NA	5.33	5.33

These data were sufficiently comparable to the vendor-supplied information to make us believe both studies were valid. We then decided to carry the studies further by reviewing monographic orders. We had the system perform a boolean search for paid monographs and had the resulting paid data displayed by country of publication according to the month the payment was made. We eliminated orders for our rare book department; in addition, we reviewed any items that cost more than $100 to attempt to verify that our database contained only the appropriate materials and that all multi-volume works were recorded at the appropriate number of volumes. Much to our displeasure, we discovered that some of the remaining records had been improperly coded and were not appropriate, thus invalidating our studies of expenditures for foreign monographs.

FIRM ORDERS/AVERAGE PAID AMOUNT PER COPY

Country	Jul-Dec 1985	Jan-Jun 1986	Jul-Dec 1986	Ave.Price % Incr.	Ave.Price % Incr. Jan-Dec.	Overall % Incr.
Britain	24.32	26.11	24.99	7.36	-4.29	2.75
Germany	21.36	27.43	30.48	28.42	11.12	42.70
Netherlands	NA	49.53	57.22	NA	15.53	15.53
Spain	18.61	20.97	29.70	12.68	41.63	59.59
France	20.24	26.61	27.93	31.47	4.96	37.99
US8	46.71	42.96	39.50	-8.03	-8.05	-15.44
US9	35.11	35.78	33.84	1.91	-5.42	-3.62
US10	12.49	25.25	23.22	102.16	-8.04	85.91
US11	NA	65.57	54.82	NA	-16.39	-16.39
US12	23.02	24.48	35.16	6.34	43.63	52.74
COMB.US	33.28	36.50	34.27	9.66	-6.09	2.98

Consequently, we did another study for the domestic materials we acquire. We buy different types of materials from the various U.S. vendors so no attempt was made to compare vendors. We simply wanted to compare data from each vendor on a month to month basis. In that second study, we looked at every individual order to see if there were reasons for the item to be excluded from the survey. In addition to eliminating rare materials, we eliminated Canadian publications and older imprints that had been ordered through U.S. vendors.

FIRM ORDERS/AVERAGE PAID AMOUNT PER COPY

Country	Jul-Sep 1985	Oct-Dec 1985	Jan-Mar 1986	Apr-Jun 1986	Jul-Sep 1986	Oct-Dec 1986	Jan 1987
US13	NA	41.20	38.73	39.20	40.43	37.95	38.83
			-6.00%	1.21%	3.14%	-6.13%	2.32%
US14	30.79	32.49	31.68	32.43	34.32	32.94	34.28
		5.52%	-2.49%	2.37%	5.83%	-4.02%	4.07%
US15	NA	19.29	20.88	22.29	21.00	21.77	20.34
			8.24%	6.75%	-5.79%	3.67%	-6.57%

Although this study also did not show the increase that we had expected, it did provide some valuable lessons regarding the difficulties of performing retrospective studies. Materials that can be cataloged quickly because there are records in our network cataloging system will be eliminated from the system database and consequently will not be reflected in any study. Our intent was to study some of the more popular scholarly works, but our results were skewed by a high percentage of the very unique, expensive or ephemeral material. We have proven to ourselves that we need to continually collect data for each separate vendor on a month to month basis, so we can analyze it whenever we wish.

Another way we attempted to compare expenditures from one year to the next was to review invoices we received from the publishers and vendors. We totaled invoices for one year from a publisher and compared the amount paid to the total paid the next year. We also counted the individual line items we paid each year to get an average cost per title. We realized that this type of study would be valid only if we were consistent in what we purchased from that source. It is an especially good kind of survey to use with some publishers like Bowker that do not sell their materials through vendors. By employing this methodology we can easily monitor the increase/decrease in Bowker titles.

One of the best means for monitoring cost increases is through the networking that we all do. By talking to vendors when they visit, to publish at various meetings, to faculty on campus and various library colleagues, one can gain valuable insight into the elements one should take into account when projecting a materials budget. It has been through this means that we have learned that many societies and associations are relying more heavily on their publishing endeavors to finance their programs. Whether we like it or not, it would appear we are subsidizing the programs of many of the organizations whose publications we buy.

Many vendors have large databases on which they operate. They, too, want to know trends in costs and are often looking for the same types of answers we seek. One foreign vendor recently sent a report of 1985 production data for the country he represents. The data were divided by subject with a breakdown by language, average cost and percent increase/decrease over the previous year. Another vendor indicated his company was monitoring differential pricing issues and foreign publishers establishing U.S. offices. With sources at hand you readily know where to turn when you want to validate any locally collected information.

Serials Studies

In the 1970s, when we were consistently monitoring material costs, we found it easy to review and compare serial costs and somewhat more difficult to compare costs for other material types. Our process for serial monitoring simply involved looking at printouts of payments for periodical titles and comparing the price increase from one year to the next. This is a sample of one of our reports from 1979.

PRICE INCREASES FOR SELECTED JOURNALS

Title	Price Increase By Per Cent	
	1971-78	1978 ONLY
Electronics Letters	329	24
Ergonomics	341	15
Journal of Chromatography	443	10

Since a favorable exchange rate and limited inflation for materials existed in the early 1980s, we did not produce reports of this kind during that time period. That fact alone is one we need to ponder. If we requested and received more funds when we wanted them in the 1970s and our purchasing power increased in the early 1980s because there was a favorable climate, should we have offered to return money to our funding agencies during this time period? Should we have brought the situation to the attention of our funding agencies with proposals for enhanced services the funds would buy? No matter what we did or should have done, we are once again in the "hat in hand" days of the 1970s. As recently reported in one of the major scientific journals:

> the cost of serials (including some books in series, such as Annual Reviews) increased by 32% from fiscal year 1985 to fiscal 1986. . . . Recent variations in the foreign-exchange rate are mainly to blame: For several years the cost in US dollars of foreign journals had remained fairly constant — in some cases even decreased — but this year the US dollar prices of some foreign journals increased dramatically; for example the cost of *Journal de Physique* increased by 69% and that of *Hyperfine Interactions* by 71%.[29]

If we were to repeat our earlier study for the serial price increases we would have a chart similar to this:

PRICE INCREASES FOR SELECTED JOURNALS

Title	Price Increase By Per Cent			
	1984	1985	1986	1987
Electronics Letters	5.1	5.2	8.7	15.5
Ergonomics	10.2	23.5	0.0	0.1
Journal of Chromatography	10.0	9.7	5.2	23.7

A study of this type, covering multi-disciplines, is often a way to convince funding sources that the total budget has been disadvantaged. Looking at this raw data alone may give a false sense of how the budget is being affected compared to the quantity or value of the material acquired. These figures do not take into consideration changes in the frequency of publication, number of pages per issue, format of the publication or its scholarly nature.

There are additional ways to examine the cost of journals and these too should be reviewed. The material itself needs to be reviewed to determine the price the publisher expects to receive. If the material is foreign, both the foreign and domestic prices are often listed in the publication. Comparing those prices with a general average rate of exchange will give a rough estimate of the effect of the differential pricing issue. Another set of interesting price data concerns publishers who list one price for institutions and another for individuals. Yet another factor to be considered is the price actually paid by the individual institution. This price will likely include postage, handling or service charges.

A detailed study comparing the cost per 1,000 characters of mathematical journals revealed significant differences among the amounts charged by various publishers. Since the publisher is listed for each title, one can easily discover that for "primary typeset journals" commercial publishers charge between 5.8 and 14.1 cents per 1,000 characters with an average cost of 9.52 cents. University produced journals ranged from 2.7 to 5.0 cents per 1,000 characters with an average of 3.78 cents. Still less expensive were the journals produced by societies and associations with a range from 1.1 to 4.4 cents per 1,000 characters and an average of 2.28 cents.[30]

The staff of the University of Michigan Library is anticipating that periodical costs may increase 17% in 1987. This increased cost has forced the staff to perform exhaustive studies which compare price changes since 1983. The studies are looking at the publisher, country of publication and the exchange rate. The studies will be used to assist the staff in working with the faculty and graduate students in a campaign to urge them to "write and complain to colleagues who serve as editors or editorial advisors for these publications and to foreign publishers in their special fields about the problem."[31]

Henry Yaple, Head of Acquisitions at the University of Wyoming, presented a paper on problem prices at the 1987 Midwinter meeting of the American Library Association. One of his illustrations was *Sun II*, a journal title which purchased from Pergamon is $425 but when purchased from the American Solar Energy Society is only $252 (member rate) or $360 (non-member rate).[32] Prices may vary considerably according to the source used to acquire the title.

CONCLUSION

Studies and reports of increased costs and the causes for the increases are important. They help us educate our clientele, make it easier for us when we try to get increased funding, and provide assistance in reviewing journals for cancellation.

There are many things we can and should do to monitor costs. We need to constantly review inflation and exchange rates. Local individual institution data should be collected systematically, even when no problem seems apparent. By collecting the data on a continuing basis, the facts and figures one needs to make informed decisions will be available when they are needed. Price index data should be compared to locally collected data to determine whether differences exist and, if so, the reasons for these differences. Knowing why these differences exist and the reasons for them can be helpful in preparing a materials funding request.

Our advice to librarians? Monitor publisher policies and their effect on you and your vendors. Listen to your vendors and the advice they have on costs. Use your network of colleagues to advise you on what they know about prices. Do all of these things consistently so that rapid changes in pricing can be known before they adversely affect materials budgets.

NOTES

1. "Book Price Decline: The Dollar Factor," *The Bookseller* (August 16, 1986):625.
2. Rich Thomas, "Double-Talk on the Dollar," *Newsweek* (February 2, 1987):45.
3. Ibid., 45.
4. Douglas Martin. "Canada Sets Tariff Retaliation: U.S. Surprised by Magnitude of the Action," *The New York Times* (June 3, 1986):D1.
5. Mary H. Loe, "Thor Tax Ruling After 5 Years: Its Effect on Publishing and Libraries," *Library Acquisitions: Practice and Theory*, 10(1986):204.

6. Michiko Kakutani, "Millions of Books Endangered as Result of Tax Ruling," *The New York Times* (October 5, 1980).

7. Marcia Tuttle, "North American Prices for British Scholarly Journals," *Library Acquisitions: Practice and Theory* 10(1986):89.

8. Ibid., 90.

9. Tuttle, "North American Prices," 93.

10. Knut Dorn and Jane Maddox, "The Acquisition of European Journals," *Library Acquisitions: Practice and Theory*, 10(1986):201.

11. Bob Schatz, "Don't Shoot the Messenger!" *Library Acquisitions: Practice and Theory*, 10(1986):85.

12. Dorn and Maddox, "Acquisition of European Journals," 202.

13. Ibid., 202.

14. Judith Niles, "Acquisitions Librarians/Vendor of Library Materials Discussion Group: ALA Midwinter Meeting, January 2, 1986," *Library Acquisitions: Practice and Theory*, 10(1986):151.

15. Undated letter from David I. Headley, Administration Director, Gordon and Breach Scientific Publishers, to Physics/Astronomy Library, University of Michigan.

16. Gayle Feldman, "Going Global," *Publisher's Weekly* (December 19, 1986):24.

17. "Publishers' Output Surges," *The Bookseller* (July 5, 1986):21.

18. Chandler B. Grannis, "U.S. Book Title Output and Average Prices, 1983-1985," *Publisher's Weekly* (October 3, 1986):90.

19. *The Bowker Annual of Library and Book Trade Information*, 30th edition (New York: R.R. Bowker Company, 1985):483.

20. Judith G. Horn, "Library Materials Price Indexes: U.S. Periodicals Preliminary Report for 1985," *RTSD Newsletter*, 10(2):19.

21. Judith G. Horn and Rebecca T. Lenzini, "Price Indexes for 1985: U.S. Periodicals," *Library Journal* 110(August 1985):54.

22. Rebecca T. Lenzini, "Periodical Prices 1984-1986 Update," *The Serials Librarian* 11 (September 1986):109.

23. Ibid., 109.

24. Ibid., 109.

25. Dora Biblarz, "Reporting Book Prices," *Book Research Quarterly*, 2(Summer 1986):83.

26. Mary E. Clack and Sally F. Williams, "Using Locally and Nationally Produced Periodical Price Indexes in Budget Preparation," *Library Resources and Technical Services* (October/December 1983):356.

27. The first year's results for Italy are omitted because of the small size of the sample.

28. The first year's results for the Dutch materials are omitted because of the small size of the sample.

29. Henry H. Barschall, "The Cost of Physics Journals," *Physics Today* (December 1986):34.

30. "Survey of American Research Journals," *American Mathematical Society, Notices* 33(March 1986):287.

31. Richard M. Dougherty, "Library to Reduce Subscriptions to Journals and Monographs," University of Michigan *University Library Update*, 3(March 1987):2.

32. Henry M. Yaple, "People in Hell Want Ice Water, Too," (Unpublished paper presented at the Resources and Technical Services Division Acquisitions Librarians/Vendors of Library Materials Discussion Group Midwinter Meeting, January 1987, Chicago, Illinois), 2.

Managing Rising Materials Costs

Frederick C. Lynden

A classic definition of management is "planning, organizing, integrating, and measuring." (1) Or said in another way: "planning, organizing and controlling." All of these facets of management should be employed in the management of Library material costs. For example, does your library have a five year plan? If it does, does that five year plan account for the materials budget in any way? Has your library organized data pertaining to materials costs in such a way that the data will provide potential for future projections? Has your library gathered all the relevant data on the prices of materials? What controls have been built into your library's materials selection process to insure avoidance of duplicates and adequate resource sharing? These are cost avoidance methods, but is your library promoting fund raising both internal and external? Has your library fostered a strong program for GOTM (Gifts other than Money)? What kind of accounting does your library have of actual materials expenditures? All of these questions emphasize the concept of establishing a comprehensive collection management program to insure that library funds for materials are justified, obtained, budgeted, and spent effectually. This paper will examine the current materials price situation for libraries, and then look at how libraries can plan and organize their collection programs to control rising materials costs. The goal of this paper will be to explore how to maximize collection buying power through the careful direction of the library's collection and acquisition programs. In the end, libraries cannot stop the costs of materials from rising, but they can minimize the effects of this cost rise by developing strategies to counteract these increases.

Frederick C. Lynden is Assistant University Librarian for Technical Services at Brown University.

CURRENT SITUATION

Inflation

According to the *Economics of Research Libraries* by Martin M. Cummings (Washington D.C. Council on Library Resources, 1986), materials expenditures at ARL libraries rose at an average annual growth rate of *4.8 percent per year* between 1961 and 1983.[2] During approximately the same period, the average price for books rose by 309 percent and the price of periodicals rose by 438 percent. The average increase for all materials was 365 percent or about 17 percent per year.[3] Libraries are clearly not keeping pace with the inflation, and a shift from expenditures for books to that of periodicals has also occurred. The effect of inflation has been a decrease in the number of book volumes and titles acquired. This decline in book acquisitions has been underway since 1972/73.

In 1974/75, according to ARL statistics, serials accounted for 48 percent of materials expenditures, and they had risen to 55 percent by 1983/84.[4]

Foreign Currency Fluctuations

In addition to inflation, libraries have had to contend with foreign currency fluctuations. Over the past seven years, the dollar has changed dramatically in relation to foreign currencies. In 1980 it was very weak, but over the next four years, it strengthened drastically. Then in 1984 it began to slide again. The following chart below shows the changes of the value of the dollar in relation to major European currencies.

U.S. Dollar Equivalent (5)

Country:	Currency:	1980:	1984:	1986 (Sept.)	1987 (Feb.)
Britain	Pound	2.3258	1.3366	1.4440	1.5200
Canada	Dollar	.8553	.7720	.7207	.7440
France	Franc	.2369	.1145	.1507	.1655
Germany	Mark	.5509	.3514	.4944	.5511
Netherlands	Guilder	.5037	.3117	.4388	.4882

As can be seen from the chart, the dollar has lost strength again, and libraries are already beginning to feel the effects. It is estimated that anywhere from 25 to 60 percent of libraries' purchases are made overseas, principally from the European countries named in the chart. When European vendors were queried about inflationary trends, they unanimously agreed that the effects of the dollar's weakness have been more deleterious to acquisition programs than has inflation. Therefore, the collection manager has to pay close attention to the foreign currency market.

Discriminatory Pricing

Another factor which has recently affected libraries purchasing heavily abroad is the discriminatory pricing controversy. According to Marcia Tuttle, who as President of the Resources and Technical Services Division visited England to discuss the discrepancy between the British domestic price for journals and the price for North American subscribers, this practice arose to recover losses from the dollar's strength, postage costs, overseas office costs, and costs for such services as 800 numbers and credit card purchases.[6] Studies by Deana Astle and Charles Hamaker as well as Siegfried Ruschin have documented the cost to American libraries. According to a follow-up study done in 1986 (two years after their first study in 1984), Astle and Hamaker concluded that "North American libraries were paying 39.3 percent more for their journals than domestic UK customers, and 18.5 percent more than "other overseas." Since the outcry from American librarians the differential has been reduced, but another publisher from Germany, Verlag Chemie (known as VCH) has joined the British publishers. Astle and Hamaker point out that of the 609 titles in 1986 published by the fifteen British publishers almost 40% have North American prices, and the average surcharge per issue in 1986 was $4.98.[7] The differential was reduced by raising the domestic prices while holding the North American price steady. Although the abstract says this paper will cover discriminatory prices, due to lack of legal restraints and inability to boycott materials, we must tolerate these increases and seek local means to control costs. So far publicity has been most effective. This paper will later suggest pre-payment discounts, elimination of duplication and increased resource sharing.

Austerity

Not only have inflation, the dollar weakness, discriminatory pricing, and increased expenditures for serials hurt libraries in terms of library materials budgets, but the general condition of austerity in higher education has been harmful to libraries seeking the necessary increase in the material budget. All institutions of higher education are facing the problems of increasing personnel costs, dwindling financial aid, greater competition for research funds, rising maintenance costs, soaring energy costs and accelerating technology costs. Tuition increases have continued to exceed the cost of living indices, and there must be efforts to attract students. As a result, the library is in competition with many other segments of the campus community, and its budgets are under scrutiny. Recently a provost at a major university responded to a plea of the university librarian for additional funds to replace the losses occurring due to the dollar downturn by sympathizing with her. At the same time, however, he said, in effect, you have benefitted by the dollar's strength and now you will have to suffer with the dollar's weakness. There is a limit to the university's ability to continue to support requests at a higher than inflationary level.

Support of Other Needs

Materials budgets are also under pressure to support other needs such as database searching, preservation, compact disk technology, electronic publishing, and video-disks. Recently there was an exchange of views on the merits of using materials funds for online services. Jay Martin Poole and Gloriana St. Clair argued in favor of using materials funds as an interim measure until other funds are available.[8] In their reaction, Sheila Dowd, John H. Whaley, Jr., and Marcia Pankake concede the need for funding of online services but questioned funding them from the materials budget. They contend that there is great overhead, that the service is individualized and not available to all, and that this type of expense belongs in the "access" or operating budget.[9] Whatever decision is made at an institution, it is clear that the materials budget is under more and more pressure to serve many purposes.

Summary

In summary, the collections are the heart of a research library. Undoubtedly this is the reason why the second highest expenditure in academic libraries, after personnel, is for materials. Currently, the materials budget is subject to some severe demands. First, inflation greater than the CPI or cost of living has made it necessary to seek large increases. Second, foreign exchange rates are decreasing the buying power of libraries overseas by as much as 35 to 40 percent. Third, in addition, discriminatory pricing has caused extra charges to be levied against the materials budget, charges which cannot be accounted for by any planning. Fourth, the materials budget is competing with other campus needs, particularly the high cost of computing and energy. Finally, new types of collections are putting additional strains on the budget since there are no other funds to support them. In view of the many demands on the materials budget, how can the collection manager/acquisitions librarian control the rising costs of materials? First, there must be a planning effort including research on costs, awareness of economic conditions, and consideration of the effects of historical and environmental variables. Second, the organization and presentation of the library's materials budget should include concern about political factors and attention to administrative considerations. Finally, there are strategies for controlling costs which comprise planning and politics, obtaining additional funds, widening cooperation with other institutions, encouraging donations in kind, and restricting costly types of expenditures.

PLANNING FOR COLLECTION BUDGETS

Published Sources

In planning for collection budgets it is very important to be aware of the trends in the costs of library materials. A first resource should be a published source of information. Anyone who reports on the price of materials to his library administration knows that the *Bowker Annual of Library and Book Trade Information* is a source of information on the prices of American books, hardcover and paperback, and American periodicals. The *Bowker Annual* also covers the prices of newspapers, media, and library produced microfilm. In addition, the prices of British academic books, German books, and Latin American books are included in the *Annual*. Currently, there is also an index for American academic books and American college books. All of these indexes are sponsored by the Library Materials Price Index Committee of the Resources Section, Resources and Technical Services Division, American Library Association, and this group can be contacted about the most up-to-date information on the prices of materials. To keep up on the trends sometimes requires reading about the price changes before they appear in the *Annual*. For example, *Publishers Weekly* carried the hardcover and paperback prices in its February or March issues and its September or October issues. Other periodicals which include early price information are *Library Journal, Serials Librarian, Library Issues: Briefings for Faculty and Administrators, the RTSD Newsletter*, and *Book Research Quarterly*. The latter contains a regular column called "Reporting Book Prices" and recently has covered such topics as German Book Prices, Foreign Book Prices, and Academic Book Prices. The Higher Education Price Index (HEPI) published by Research Associates, Washington, D.C., is also useful as a documentation of trends in the price of books, serials, and foreign books shown in relation to each other. Finally, ALANET, ALA's electronic mail system, will soon include information on periodical prices to update information appearing in *LJ*.

Book or Periodical Vendor

A second resource on trends is the book or periodical vendor. Most collection managers are aware that vendors will often provide institution-specific cost data. For example, for many years now F.W. Faxon, Inc. has made available, for a fee, a three year comparative study of the prices of periodicals purchased by local institutions. Many approval plan vendors provide such cost data on books supplied to a particular institution. All of these studies are produced as a by-product of the vendor's computerized data. In addition to these local studies, vendors are now publishing national price studies based upon the titles supplied to academic libraries. The academic index referred to earlier is based upon the studies of the following vendors: Baker and Taylor, Blackwell North America, Yankee and Coutts. Vendor price studies have some advantages over the general price indexes included in the *Bowker Annual* since they are selective, contain up-to-date price information, and tend to report fiscal year data. Frequently these vendor studies provide the only information which can be obtained on the "academic sub-set" of price data for library materials. My research has indicated that vendor price data is a very promising source for foreign academic price data.

Local Cost Study

A third resource for establishing trends is a local cost study. Nothing substitutes for this type of study. One of the earliest local studies was done at Stanford University Library. This study tracked the average costs of American university press and approval titles, foreign blanket orders, and serials. Serial expenditure rates are particularly important to measure since serials tend to rise at a faster rate than monographs and usually include the largest part of expenditures. The Stanford study was a manually produced study, but it is now possible to keep very detailed data using local computer systems. ARL has documented the variety of local cost studies in an ARL SPEC kit. One recent presentation by a librarian from Michigan State demonstrated how her local ćommercial computer system could show average cost data by geographic region, subject, format, vendor or country. The system can calculate average price data and show all of the results in tabular form. As has been noted many times before, there is no substitute for local data presented to a budgeting authority. At the same time, it is advisable to show how the local data relates to trends for other academic libraries. In order to do this, one must be aware of the published indexes which are available. A current example of the value of such cross-checks is the experience of the British Academic Book Price Index. Until recently it was compiled using data from the *British National Bibliography*. Books supplied on copyright deposit to the Cambridge University Library provided the raw data for the study, and the prices were obtained from the *BNB*. It was discovered in 1982/83 that the general indexes were showing increases while the ABPI was reflecting a decrease. Further research showed that the *BNB* was not reporting prices on 44 percent of its records. Another flaw in the *BNB* as a source of price information was the inclusion of many imprints from years prior to 1982/83 due to the processing of a cataloging backlog.[10] Needless to say, the ABPI is now using vendor data.

Historical and Environmental Variables

As part of planning one must also consider the effects of historical and environmental variables. When planning for a materials budget, one must, for example, take account of such factors as "the users — faculty, graduate students, and undergraduates; special faculty research interests; new programs; research grants available; and local resource sharing arrangements." These factors naturally affect the size, the scope, and sources of the budget. First, the size can be influenced by grants. If the budget has been supported by grants in a specific area and these grants are diminished without any replacement funds, then the overall budget will be reduced in size. Second, the scope can be modified by other factors. The extent of the budget will also be affected by the user population, faculty research interests, and new programs. If a university is supporting a graduate program in

West European studies, then the budget will need to maintain purchases from West European nations, an expensive proposition as could be seen from the changes in the exchange rates. Finally, the budget planner must be aware of potential funding sources. If a faculty member receives a special research grant, might there be funds to share with the library? Historical factors come into play when one examines past budgets. Perhaps the argument should be made that a library should get more than an inflationary increase due to past inequities in funding support for collections. Historical resource sharing arrangements will also determine where costs can be avoided. At Duke and North Carolina, for example, where regional French history is collected cooperatively, the libraries of each institution have settled on specific geographic regions in which one collects and the other does not. This allows in-depth purchases without cutting into funds for other parts of the collection program.

In summary, planning for a materials budget requires the following steps. First, one must measure the changes in local materials expenditures. Second, one must compare these changes with national trends, using vendor data where possible. Third, vendor data which is institutional specific can provide strength to a library's case. Fourth, additional factors to consider beyond inflationary trends are retrospective (historical) collection needs; new program requirements, including level of materials required; extent of foreign materials required; and special arrangements among institutions for sharing collecting responsibilities. Finally, planning should include attention to the possible internal and external sources of funding.

ORGANIZATION AND PRESENTATION OF THE MATERIALS BUDGET

Marketing a Materials Budget

It is important to organize efforts to sell the materials budget to the administration. There are several elements to marketing a materials budget. First, regular communication with campus officials is a necessary part of selling the budget. There should be no surprises for the administration. For example, it does not hurt to keep the administration informed about what the changes in the value of the dollar overseas are doing to the book and serials budget. Indeed it is useful to keep all campus constituencies informed about what is happening to collection expenditures through articles in the campus daily, alumni magazine, and newsletter as well as regular informal and formal memos to principal campus officers such as the dean, the provost, and the Vice-President for Business and Finance. Second, alliances with faculty can be useful before making the budget presentation. In many academic institutions, a faculty committee is concerned with library activities and policies, and it is important to keep this group apprised of the economic situation as it relates to materials expenditures. These people can then become significant allies when a budget presentation is made. It is 'also not unusual for faculty to play a major role in approving a campus budget, and well placed friends of the library can be of great assistance at the right moment.

Third, another political factor in convincing the administration of the library's needs is credibility. If the library has always been honest in presenting a materials budget, there will be times when the inflationary rate is lower and the library must be up-front about the possibility of reducing support. (Of course, in these cases honesty and frankness can be accompanied by a list of retrospective needs!) Fourth, the tone, the clarity, and brevity of the actual request are factors in making the request more palatable. Bad news well presented can be more acceptable than good news badly communicated. Indeed the proposal need not be as detailed if the administration is already well informed about the economic situation. In this respect, it is worth mentioning that *Library Issues: Briefings for Faculty and Administrators* contains regular articles on the costs of materials, preservation, and automation. More recently this newsletter has had articles on the value of the dollar, called the "Dollar Watch."[11] Finally, it is important for the Library to be very aware of institutional politics and priorities. For example, when one's university is intending to apply for an NEH grant, the library should be the first to make its needs known. On the other hand, if the local priority is financial aid, then the library may wish to keep a low profile and understate its case thus assuring passage of a "modest" request.

Administrative Considerations

There are also administrative considerations when presenting a materials budget to local authorities: "the local cycle for requests; staff participation; presentation of the request; endowment and gift funds; serial vs. book funds; pressure from other parts of the library budget; and fund raising and allocations." First, the local cycle makes it necessary for one to know when data is available. Until recently, general serial price data for the calendar year was not available until July or August. It is now available as early as April in the *Library Journal*.

The collection manager must know when national data is available to plan properly for the request. Second, it is helpful to increase staff participation in the budgeting process because staff may have creative ideas on funding as well as know specific sources of income for collection development. Third, in the presentation of the budget, the most common form of request is a percentage increase to maintain the budget, based on inflationary rates, but there are many other approaches which will help to increase the funding received and reduce the impact of rising costs:

1. Additional funds requested for new programs;
2. Funds for retrospective purchases;
3. Special funds to compensate for the dollar weakness;
4. Monies for expensive purchases which could not be made;
5. Budget base increase requests to make up for previous austerity;
6. Special allocations to keep up with the number of new publications;
7. Extra monies to increase the number of volumes received;
8. Accounting for differential rates required to fund different formats.

All of these approaches require documentation, and the time required for preparation of such documentation must be taken into consideration as one organizes the budget presentation. Fourth, the collection manager must be very aware of the expenditure components of the budget, i.e., what is being spent from general funds, gifts, and endowments; what is used for serials versus monographs; and what pressures there are from other segments of the budget, especially automation. For example, knowledge of these components then makes it possible to ask for more income from endowments when the general funds are low or to suggest additional general (institutional) funds for library automation to relieve pressure on the materials budget. Finally, if the library has its budget presentation well organized, it is possible to tell what areas required the most funding in past years, and this information permits fund raising with specific targets to occur. Furthermore, allocations can aid the budget planner in organizing support for the budget. If the history faculty is aware that past allocations have been inadequate, then this faculty can become a significant ally in the arguments for increasing the budget for library materials. In this instance, allocations become the evidence for greater support. The faculty members can provide information about unfilled requests, the lack of major microform purchases, missed retrospective purchases, and other special needs which have gone wanting.

In summary, skillful organization and presentation can set the stage for controlling materials costs. Organizing one's justification for the materials budget requires effective communication and political skills. It is important to keep the campus community informed about the costs of materials, and it is equally important for the collection manager to be aware of what is happening on campus as it might affect the library's budget. It is also useful to have allies among the institution's faculty and administration to know who is sympathetic to the library's causes. And the library must be consistently honest in its appraisals of materials costs. Presentation of the budget depends not only on integrity but also hard work, good research, staff participation, and a thorough knowledge of local policies and priorities. The groundwork for controlling costs relies on superb planning and organization.

CONTROLLING LIBRARY MATERIALS COSTS

As noted earlier, in economic terms it is really not possible to control library materials costs since library materials are the raw materials for libraries and their costs are determined by factors outside of the library's control. Therefore, economies can come only from reducing expenditures for library materials or raising revenues to keep up with inflation. Occasionally we have seen consumer action result in publishers holding their prices, but rarely is it possible to boycott the product, and that is usually done only when another copy is available elsewhere. Substitution of less costly formats such as microforms is one possibility. In the *Economics of Research Libraries*, Martin M. Cummings suggests three methods of controlling increased materials costs:

> One obvious approach is to diminish the rate of acquisition and/ or reduce the number of duplicate copies of an item held. Decreasing purchases of new materials results in direct cost savings but also in narrower coverage of subject areas. Reducing the number of copies of an item limits availability of material. It may be that lessening the length of loan periods would increase the availability of materials with less adverse impact than other solutions. However, if the cost of user time in obtaining information is considered this is a poor strategy. Another option available for controlling materials costs is to engage in resource sharing.[12]

To these three strategies: reducing acquisitions, eliminating duplicates, and resource sharing, one should add fund raising; encouragement of gifts (in kind); improved budget requests; and improved acquisition practices. These strategies will be covered under five rubrics: *Planning* and the political process; the *outside* development process; *widening* cooperation; *economical* acquisition processes; and *reduction* of acquisitions.

PLANNING AND THE POLITICAL PROCESS

Budget justification is one means of controlling costs because an institution which keeps pace with the rising costs of materials has the situation under control. the elements of planning for a budget presentation have already been mentioned, but the factors which are convincing to administrators have not been noted. In 1978, there was research done on what exactly is convincing to administrators. According to this research administrators are best persuaded by: (1) maintenance of buying power despite inflation; (2) relation of budgetary arguments to research and teaching; (3) alliances with faculty and the deans; (4) integrity of the presentation and the presenter, i.e., credibility of the proposed budget and the library budget manager; and (5) external evidence such as rankings. These elements inspire confidence from the university administration. Another important contributor to confidence is long range planning. The administration can then be aware in advance about the type of expenditures one might expect. Harvard University Library issued a ten year plan in 1966 which predicted massive expenditures for materials in 1976/77 as well as additional space needs, greater reliance on computers, and increased use of microforms.[13] When there are fewer surprises, large budgets become much more tolerable. The Harvard approach in materials budget justification as documented by Sally F. Williams, Associate Librarian for Financial Affairs, includes keeping the budget proposal "simple, salient, scrupulous, with no surprises."[14]

Two approaches to budget justification which have been very successful in convincing administrative authorities to meet inflationary needs were reported in *LRTS* in 1983. The library administration of the University of California system uses the price indexes reported in the *Bowker Annual* for its annual prognostications of materials prices. Using a three-year geometric mean price increase, subject by subject, the budget is derived by multiplying the average price increase (over three years) against the expenditures for monographs, serials, and serials services. This formula has proven successful in obtaining requisite funds for materials expenditures at the University of California. [15] At Harvard, the central library administration uses a combination of published sources and local data. In the case of the latter, the information is automated, both from the university financial system and in-house reports from local acquisition system. Using expenditure and budget report information from the past three fiscal years, the library administration is able to estimate a projected increase. The price index data is presented "along with any special considerations of changes in the scope of the collection or significant changes in funding (such as loss of a government contract)." [16] According to the compiler, Sally F. Williams, "one of the persuasive sources of information was the index of Effective Exchange Rate published by the International Monetary Fund in its periodical *International Financial Statistics*." [17] The above two approaches show that published and local data, some long term analysis, and special considerations should always be a part of materials budget presentations.

One of the frustrating aspects of doing excellent materials budget presentations can be a lack of success not because a presentation was not convincing but because the institution simply could not raise the funds to support paying for double digit inflation. The argument has been made that there is no need for elaborate preparation and presentation of the materials budget. This work, the argument goes, is wasted effort. On the contrary, politically this viewpoint is seriously flawed. Most university administrations have some very good funding years and some very poor funding years and many in-between, and the budget presenter if she/he has been consistent in providing reliable data can call upon the university during the good years to make up for previous inadequate budgets. For example, when the university's financial health is good, then it is time to request funds for retrospective purchases. If past budget requests have been well documented, then some expensive purchase lists from past years can be included. Documentation of needs is never lost effort.

One approach which Brown intends to take for improving budgets for materials is linking the materials budget requests to the university's energy request. Specifically, Brown hopes to persuade the university to support serials budgets as they do special energy costs. Universities must pay for energy costs or they would have to shut down. They should protect library resources in the same way. Library resources are essential to the functioning of the academic machine. When outside forces cause the costs to escalate, the library cannot simply forego journal subscriptions. It is not possible to immediately cancel serial subscriptions, therefore, the university should provide special support for continuations during "difficult" periods, e.g., during a dollar downturn. Once the principle of giving special support for serial price fluctuations is established, then the materials budget will be much stronger since serial costs are clearly one of the price rise areas most difficult to control.

THE OUTSIDE DEVELOPMENT PROCESS

Every library, by now, has recognized the need for outside fund raising. One of the most attractive "opportunities" for donors is contributing to collections. Strong gift and endowment support for collections can be a positive antidote to the reduction of general funds, but there must be an organized effort to increase these funds. Gifts, grants, and fees make up an important share of the acquisition dollars, and they come from a variety of sources. There are several ways of raising such funds: friends' groups, development campaigns, grant proposals, fines, and sale of services. It is important to have library staff give attention to fund raising to insure that revenues are received.

Friends groups can provide the impetus for collection fund raising. Some novel techniques have been employed by friends groups including a shopping list of titles and their prices in a library newsletter for the friends; sales of Christmas cards and note paper; leaflets to describe what contributions can do; acting as a recipient for a gift in a state university (thus avoiding legal prohibitions against future sales); and advertising needs in specially printed annual reports for friends. In addition to a friends group, the library frequently has a staff member assigned to development efforts and grant proposals. In a survey of twelve private university libraries almost ten years ago, half of the libraries had appointed a staff member whose responsibility it was to seek funds from outside sources. At Brown, the Assistant University Librarian for Special Collections has been working half-time in the Development Office for the past nine months, and this has resulted in realizing receipt of the full amount of NEH challenge funds with two years still left in the challenge period. His reassignment was made in order to capitalize on a $750,000 challenge grant from the National Endowment for the Humanities which will support collection funds for materials in the humanities. At the twelve private libraries, two of the six staff assigned to fund raising activities were full-time staff members, and the four others held part-time fund raising positions. In all cases, there is close coordination with the campus development office. This insures that the library is made an active part of university fund-raising campaigns. As one director put it: "Fund raisers cannot be as enthusiastic and knowledgeable as librarians."[18]

ARL libraries now charge fees for services in such areas as online searching, current awareness, interlibrary loan, photoduplication, microform duplication, and external user borrowing. In the future, it is also expected that fees will pay partially or fully for online services if a user requests an individual print-out or some specialized search which is not available to all users. Many of these accounts are "wash" accounts. In the case of fines for lost books, it is assumed that the monies will pay for replacement books or substitutes so there is no real gain. Many libraries use the average cost of a hardcover book (now $31.46) and a processing charge when fining the patron. In any case, it should be the long range objective to charge more than costs in collection related areas in order to supplement the collection budget.

WIDENING COOPERATION

In addition to obtaining extra funds to pay for increases, materials costs can be controlled by widening cooperative arrangements, i.e., increasing access rather than acquisition. Resource sharing will help control costs, not reduce them, because resource sharing aids libraries in avoiding costs. As Scott Bennett has said, "The reality is that librarians are pursuing cooperative collection management (just as they have pursued automation) not to reduce costs but to improve services."[19] Cost avoidance is best achieved through coordinated collection building. A prime example, often cited, is the coordinated efforts between the University of North Carolina and Duke. Recently a bibliographer at University of North Carolina described how the two libraries have divided the responsibilities for collection of French regional history geographically. The program is well accepted by the faculty because only third priority materials are included in the program. The collecting agreements permit the libraries to acquire materials in the desired depth without requiring sacrifices in other subject areas. It is possible to build a major collection of French regional history with each institution only paying half the costs.[20] However, to do this requires an excellent delivery system and a detailed knowledge of each collection.

Another step libraries can take is to improve interlibrary loan service so that it is possible to increase the access to other collections. The lag time in delivery of interlibrary loans is frequently an impediment to faculty use. At Brown, through a combination of steps, the interlibrary loan fill time has been cut down to an average of nine days using computer communication and UPS delivery service. Delivery service was recently the focus of grants from the Fred Meyer Charitable Trust of The Pacific Northwest. The Meyer program, Library and Information Resources for the Northwest (LIRN), made $736,000 available to five libraries for innovative document delivery pilot systems using satellite teletext, optical scanning, and telefacsimile based document delivery.[21] These libraries are testing what will be the future modes of document delivery.

Another element in improving cooperation is the definition of collecting areas. An important tool for identifying collection strengths and weaknesses is the RLG Conspectus which has been adopted as the principal tool of the North American Collections Inventory Project. The conspectus is arranged by subject according to the LC classification, and libraries use standard codes to indicate the strength of collections and the level of current acquisitions. Other notes show language coverage and special strengths. In December 1985, the Fred Meyer Trust appointed a task force to develop profiles of collections in the Pacific Northwest. This task force employed the RLG methodology in the first efforts to devise coordinated collection programs and document delivery. In January 1987, the Fred Meyer Trust announced seventeen grants totalling $1.6 Million to develop coordinated programs to build collections in the Pacific Northwest. For each grant there is a lead organization and cooperating organizations. For example, the University of the Puget Sound is working with Pacific Lutheran University, St. Martin's College, Seattle Pacific University, and Seattle University "to *jointly* build a wide range of printed and computerized information resources to support undergraduate and graduate programs in education." The grant was for $225,000 over three years. The program is designed, as noted by Douglas K. Ferguson, Director of LIRN, to create "models of cooperation for more effective buying in the face of rising demand and stable or declining budgets for library collections."[22]

ENCOURAGE GOTM (GIFTS OTHER THAN MONEY) AND ECONOMICAL COLLECTION PROCESSES

Another measure in controlling library costs is to promote an effective program for encouraging gifts of materials. It is important for a library to have a librarian dedicated to the solicitation, acceptance and processing of gifts. Libraries should also have policies for acceptance and disposal of gifts. The disposal of gifts may result in revenues through sales. Indeed, investment in a gift program can mean dividends of both cash and public relations. Gift programs should also include efforts to foster donors. How aware is the library of editors of major journals on campus? Frequently such journals review books and books not reviewed are disposed of. What contacts does the library have with local diplomatic missions? Often foreign government agencies hope to encourage an understanding of their country through donations of library materials. What can the Friends Group do to identify major collectors among their ranks? All of the above elements can contribute to an active gift program.

Acceptance of gifts is crucial to the success of a program which encourages gifts. Most libraries which have successful programs have liberal acceptance policies. That is not to say that libraries should not have provisions for disposal of unwanted materials, but rather that some chaff must be accepted along with the wheat in order to get a bountiful harvest. Indeed the regulations for acceptance should include the right to dispose of materials. If these provisions are not made clear from the beginning, then the entire gift program can be damaged. Proper acknowledgement can also insure continued giving. Good public relations can sustain a giving program, and part of good public relations includes giving attention to the donor and the gift. This means processing the materials with alacrity. Processing speed can also determine savings. For example, current gifts containing current imprints should be processed prior to receipt of ordered current imprints in order to gain maximum benefit from a current imprint gift program. When an effective gift program is maintained, the savings and revenues can aid substantially in offsetting the rising costs of materials.

Economical collection processes refer to both improvements in the collection techniques (which do not necessarily translate into savings for purchases) as well as a consideration of the economics of collection building. In the former case, other conference presentations have given good evidence for the value of gathering plans and standing orders in any acquisition program. These programs hold down costs by insuring prompt receipt of new titles (avoiding costly out-of-print searches) reducing searching costs (avoiding expensive staff costs), and eliminating typing of process slips (avoiding costs of typing slips) as well as savings in selector collection work. Another creative approach which vendors recommend as an antidote to higher serials costs is taking advantage of vendor pre-payment plans when purchasing serials. B.H. Blackwell, Harrassowitz, and Nijhoff offer from 5 to 8 percent discounts for pre-paying early invoices for serials. These plans offer an advantage to the vendor because the vendor can be assured of a sale and earn interest on the deposited monies. But libraries can realize savings as well. This appears to be a very promising approach to controlling costs. According to the book by Cummings, one economic factor which is often not considered is the use which a volume receives. He notes:

> Since the collection may be considered a major capital asset, one measure of cost effectiveness is the total value of the capital asset divided by the total units of use. Since the older portion of the collection has a lower rate of use, there is a downward pressure: cost-effectiveness decreases as the collection increases. This requires the librarian to serve as a capital assets manager in controlling costs and stimulating use of the collection.[23]

Cummings goes on to point out that collection managers should avoid buying little used materials but instead arrange for access to them. Another approach along these lines is to encourage use of the collections which an institution has through advertising their availability in bibliographic utilities, book catalogs, and in specialized catalogs. Several years ago, the Council on Library Resources (CLR) offered grants to scholars to visit collections. Rather than bringing collections to the scholar, CLR had a program for bringing the scholars to the collections.

REDUCTION OF ACQUISITIONS

As with all of the steps involved in controlling the costs of materials, there must be careful planning. Planning is particularly important in reducing acquisitions. One prime example should be given. At this moment, due to the falling value of the dollar against foreign currencies, serials budgets have been particularly hard hit. At ALA Midwinter, a number of librarians were talking about losing $100,000 to $300,000 this year due to serial price increases. In order to plan for these events, libraries must have lists of serials they are prepared to cancel: e.g., must have, important, marginal. Since cancellations cannot be done in mid-year without tremendous processing costs, it is clear that advance planning must take place. Furthermore, faculty should have already been consulted, otherwise collection "damage" cannot be minimized. Reduction of acquisitions should include restricting the purchases of duplicates, expensive items, and serials. Collection development policies can also help focus buying and avoid unnecessary purchases.

Most libraries, by now, have eliminated duplicate serial titles and have asked selectors to avoid duplicate monographic purchases (except where required for readers). Surprisingly, libraries with multiple branches still maintain duplicate subscriptions, and it is not until faculty are made very aware of the costs (in terms of other titles which cannot be obtained) that they agree to cancellations. The local delivery capabilities are also a key to the willingness to cancel. In a study of twelve private university libraries, seven of the twelve libraries had restrictions, including a stringent review, on expensive purchases. Six of the twelve libraries had systems for controlling the growth of expenditures for serials. All of the libraries had policies on duplication which amounted to avoidance of duplication except when required for research or teaching.[24] Many libraries have developed forms which require documentation of the decision to purchase serials and expensive items. These forms frequently require written justification for the purchase including signatures of faculty members and the university librarian.

A review of requests for serials is a rather significant factor in controlling the costs of serials because in most research libraries serials expenditures amount to more than fifty percent of the entire materials budget. This problem is really an international one. In September 1986 the International Publishers Association sent out the following announcement:

> Decrease in library budgets for acquisition of books, periodicals, and other carriers of information has been noticeable in several countries in recent years.
> In some libraries, particularly in specialized and university libraries, funds were transferred from books to periodicals buying. On the whole, however, decrease in book buying was not compensated by periodical or other carriers buying.
> IPA wishes to draw the attention of national and regional authorities on the damaging trend of declining library budgets for education, research and public information.
> IPA members are kindly requested to provide statistical data on library buying during three following years, as recent as possible.[25]

A serials purchase is a long term commitment which involves not only subscription costs but also binding costs. There are also a myriad number of processing costs from claiming and check-in to invoice payment. Furthermore, the rate of serial inflation is sufficiently high that if serial subscriptions are kept static and the materials budget increases at rates lower than inflation, the monographic budget will gradually be reduced to next to nothing. Such a serious state of affairs demands a careful scrutiny of all serial purchase requests.

CONCLUSIONS

Management of rising materials costs requires a plan of action which incorporates the following elements:

— A record of the trends in the costs of materials from publishers, vendors, and the American Library Association Library Materials Price Index Committee.
— Data on changes in local materials expenditures, including a breakdown by subject, country, and format.
— Information about library users, new university programs, rates of worldwide publication, rates of acquisition at other institutions, foreign exchange rates, and special collection responsibilities.
— A strategy for marketing the budget request based on a knowledge of local politics and policies, including historical background of the institution.
— An approach which documents needs in a clear, crisp, and concise fashion which is understandable to budgeting authorities.
— Persuasive arguments which relate budgetary needs to university programs of instruction and research.
— A development program which includes an active Friends group, library staff assigned to development, and a campaign for library funds.
— Full participation in resource sharing activities such as collection inventories, an efficient interlibrary loan program, and collection coordination.
— Promotion of gifts other than money (gifts in kind) through proper staffing, processing, and public relations.
— Restrictions on the purchase of expensive materials, serials, and duplicates through formal programs of review and justification.

To develop these elements into a cohesive program for controlling costs requires active staff involvement in planning and implementation. These elements cannot become a blueprint for action unless there is hard work done to document costs, market the library's needs, promote external gifts of funds and materials, and encourage full participation in resource sharing. To accomplish this work, there should be a collection budget group which includes such staff as the collection development officer, the acquisition and serials librarians, the library business manager, the library fund raiser, and the university librarian. With clear goals and the necessary expertise, it will be possible to achieve a program for managing rising materials costs.

NOTES

1. Peter F. Drucker, *Management: Tasks, Responsibilities and Practices*, (New York, Harper & Row Publishers, 1973), p. 393.

2. Martin M. Cummings, *Economics of Research Libraries*, (Washington, D.C., Council on Library Resources, 1986), p. 146-148.

3. Kent D. Halstead, *Inflation Measures for Schools and Colleges*, (Washington, D.C., Department of Education, September 1983), p. 80.

4. Cummings, *Op. Cit*. p. 19-20.

5. "Dollar Watch: Foreign Currencies and the Declining Purchasing Power of the Dollar," *Library Issues*, vol. 6, no. 4:3-4. (1986).

6. Marcia Tuttle, "The Pricing of British Journals for the North American Market," *Library Resources and Technical Services* 30:72-78 (January/March 1986).

7. Deana Astle and Charles Hamaker, "Pricing by Geography: British Journal Pricing 1986, Including Developments in Other Countries," *Library Acquisitions Practice and Theory*, vol. 10: 170 (1986).

8. Jay Martin Poole and Gloriana St. Clair, "Funding Online Services from the Materials Budget," *College and Research Libraries* 47:229 (May 1986).

9. Sheila Dowd, John H. Whaley and Marcia Pankake, "Reactions to Funding Online Services from the Materials Budget," *College and Research Libraries* 47:230-237 (May 1986).

10. Peter H. Mann, "Library Acquisitions: the Economic Constraints," *The Bookseller* 4199: 2340 (June 14, 1986).

11. "Dollar Watch . . . ," *Op. Cit*.

12. Cummings, *Op. Cit.*, p. 150.

13. *The Harvard University Library, 1966-1976, Report of a Planning Study Submitted to the President by the Director of the University Library and the University Librarian*, (Cambridge, MA, Harvard University Library, May 1966).

14. Sally F. Williams, "Budget Justification: Closing the Gap between Request and Result," *Library Resources and Technical Services* 28:134 (April/June 1984).

15. Dennis Smith, "Forecasting Price Increase Needs for Library Materials: the University of California Experience," *Library Resources and Technical Services* 28:136-148 (April/June 1984).

16. Williams, *Op. Cit.*, p. 133.

17. *Ibid*.

18. Frederick C. Lynden, "External Fund-Raising for Book Fund (A CLR Fellowship Report)," in *ARL SPEC Kit Number 48*, (Washington, D.C., Association of Research Libraries, 1978.)

19. Scott Bennett, "Current Initiatives and Issues in Collection Management," *Journal of Academic Librarianship*, 10:257-261 (November 1984).

20. John Rutledge, "Collecting French Regional History Cooperatively," *Collection Management* 8:63-77 (Summer 1986).

21. "$1.6 Million in Grants to Improve Library Collections," *Press Release* from the Fred Meyer Charitable Trust, Portland Oregon, January 2, 1987.

22. *Ibid*.

23. Cummings, *Op. Cit.*, p. 112-114.
24. Frederick C. Lynden, "Library Materials Budgeting in the Private University Library: Austerity and Action," *Advances in Librarianship* 10:90-154 (1980).
25. "Library Book and Periodical Spending," Letter of June 16, 1986.

BIBLIOGRAPHY

Astle, Deana and Hamaker, Charles, "Pricing by Geography: British Journal Pricing 1986, Including Developments in "Other Countries," *Library Acquisitions Practice and Theory*, vol. 10: 165-181 (1986).

Bennett, Scott "Current Initiatives and Issues in Collection Management," *Journal of Academic Librarianship*, 10:257-261 (November 1984).

Cummings, Martin M. *Economics of Research Libraries*, (Washington, D.C., Council on Library Resources, 1986), 216 p.

"Dollar Watch: Foreign Currencies and the Declining Purchasing Power of the Dollar," *Library Issues, vol. 6, no. 4:3-4. (1986).*

Dowd, Sheila, Whaley, John H., and Pankake, Marcia, "Reactions to Funding Online Services from the Materials Budget," *College and Research Libraries* 47:230-237 (May 1986).

Drucker, Peter F. *Management: Tasks, Responsibilities and Practices*, (New York, Harper and Row Publishers, 1973), 839 p.

Halstead, Kent D. *Inflation Measures for Schools and Colleges*, (Washington, D.C. Department of Education, September 1983).

The Harvard University Library, 1966-1976, Report of a Planning Study. Submitted to the President by the Directory of the University Library and the *University Librarian*, (Cambridge, MA, Harvard University Library, May 1966).

International Publisher's Association. "Library Book and Periodical Spending," Letter of June 16, 1986.

Lynden, Frederick C. "Library Materials Cost Studies," *Library Resources and Technical Services* 27:156-162 (April/June 1983).

Lynden, Frederick C. "External Fund-Raising for Book Fund (ACRL Fellowship Report), in *ARL SPEC Kit Number* 48, (Washington, D.C., Association of Research Libraries, 1978).

Lynden, Frederick C. "Financial Planning for Collection Management," *Journal of Library Administration* 3:109-120 (Fall/Winter 1982).

Lynden, Frederick C. "Library Materials Budgeting in the Private University Library: Austerity and Action," *Advances in Librarianship* 10:90-154 (1980).

Mann, Peter H. "Library Acquisitions: the Economic Constraints," *The Bookseller* 2340: 4199 (June 14, 1986).

"$1.6 Million in Grants to Improve Library Collections," *Press Release* from the Fred Meyer Charitable Trust, Portland, Oregon, January 2, 1987.

Poole, Jay Martin and St. Clair, Gloriana, "Funding Online Services from the Materials Budget," *College and Research Libraries* 47:225-229 (May 1986).

Rutledge, John "Collecting French Regional History Cooperative," *Collection Management* 8:63-77 (Summer 1986).

Smith, Dennis "Forecasting Price Increase Needs for Library Materials: the University of California Experience," *Library Resources and Technical Services* 28:136-148 (April/June 1984).

Tuttle, Marcia "The Pricing of British Journals for the North American Market," *Library Resources and Technical Services* 30:72-78 (January/March 1986).

Williams, Sally F. "Budget Justification: Closing the Gap between Request and Result," *Library Resources and Technical Services* 28:129-135 (April/June 1984).

CD-ROM, Databases,
and Other New Information Formats:
Their Acquisition

Jennifer Cargill

As we plan our tactics for surviving these times of financial retrenchment, still another issue must be added to our growing list of considerations when we are dealing with budgeting constraints.

Libraries have traditionally focused on the acquisitions of materials in paper format—books and periodicals—or in microform. Though there has been resistance to the use of microforms, we have found an increasing number of publications, including entire sets, are primarily available in microformat. Use of microforms has been for basically three reasons: space conservation, preservation of materials, and access. As access has become increasingly self service, this direct user access has in turn escalated as information has become such an important and highly desirable commodity. Ease and comfort of access has also become an issue.

During the 1980s, information has become available in an increasing variety of media as technological advances have reached the marketplace. Still developing technologies promise to provide even more means of distributing and easily accessing information. Now—and into the future—access to information will cease being dependent upon the printed or microformat page.

Online databases are accessible within the library setting and from the microcomputer or terminal housed in the user's workplace. Printed indexes, housed on rows of index tables, now are available online or on CD-ROM, accessible through use of a microcomputer. A popular example is the fairly recent introduction of InfoTrac, a database stored on videodisc, that is already available in more than 300 libraries.

With this development of new technologies, libraries will be acquir-

Jennifer Cargill is Associate Director of Libraries for Information Access and Systems at Texas Tech University.

ing, accessing, and distributing information in many of these new media. Historically, libraries have been extremely format conscious. We have been insistent on retaining format distinctions within our collections. With the new technologies, with the explosion of types of information storage media, will we continue to be so format conscious? Will we balk at the increased acquisition of databases on videodisc, CD-ROM, or floppy discs? Will we resist acquiring these databases on our materials budget? Will we argue against using the same funds for purchasing these new formats as those we use to acquire books, serials, and microforms?

While it is unlikely that we will become a paperless society, we *will* become increasingly reliant upon electronic means to acquire and retain information. Libraries will be able to move away from warehousing quantities of materials to an emphasis on acquisition and dissemination of information using different modes, including remote access. We must begin thinking of the acquisitions funds as the information resources budget, and not as a budget earmarked solely for more traditional formats. We will begin to see the focus becoming the more effective access *to* and dissemination *of* information.

As librarians we always remember our role in providing access to information and assistance in providing this effective access *to* and utilization *of* that information. The client, whether a sophisticated researcher or a novice, is concerned with obtaining the information. In the past we could direct him or her to hard copy indexes, to books in the stacks, or to periodicals, either in hard copy or in microform. Earlier I mentioned our historical concern with format. Now with the new media for housing information, we are again focusing on a concern for format. But the information itself is the critical ingredient, not how it is stored. We must be willing to expend our information resources on obtaining access to information.

In the past we have used our funds for obtaining and retaining information in traditional formats. When we purchase books or periodicals, we are purchasing what we think is needed and gambling that it will indeed be used. When we spend funds for online access or for the purchase of a database, we are acquiring an item that will potentially provide information tailored to a client's needs. As Poole and St. Clair argue in a recent article, online access is similar to purchasing materials for reserve, for specific research, or for interlibrary loan.

New methods for acquiring and storing information include CD-ROM, videodisc, and floppy disk. Some media provide access to large databases; others provide a convenient means of access to an existing work.

Let us first review some of the types of new information storage media about which we are concerned. CD-ROM is an example of this new media. It is a compact disk, read only memory, meaning it can be read but that additional data cannot be added, reorganized, or erased. Technology that originally created a medium to provide flawless musical sounds has been extended to provide storage for microcomputer programs and databases. That storage capacity is such that on a disk weighing less than an ounce can be stored 275,000 pages or the equivalent of 1,500 floppy disks.

Databases stored on CD-ROM cover many subject areas including Chemistry, Engineering, Law and Public Policy, Medicine, and library and information science. In all there are around 100 CD-ROM titles available in 21 subject categories. One of the most popular CD-ROM applications is for library and information science; one-quarter of the CD-ROM databases are in the library field. These library and information science products are for two potential uses:

1. databases for information retrieval for clients; and
2. databases for routine library applications such as acquisitions and cataloging.

As we acquire these CD-ROM databases for library or patron use, we face some concerns for compatibility; standards are being developed, both physical standards — recently introduced — and data format standards. Cost and availability are other factors. A recent study indicated 92% of U.S. libraries did not own CD-ROM players. Of those which have none, 67% had no immediate plans to acquire a CD-ROM player. Of those with players, 72% of their use was by library staff only, suggesting use for bibliographic data retrieval for library functional activities. Of course, with the increasing availability of databases on CD-ROM, the number of players in libraries is likely to change dramatically.

One of the most widely used and popular databases using some of the new technology is InfoTrac, a system using videodiscs as the storage media. Its entry into library reference departments has been the subject of some controversy since its coverage is limited and some libraries have experienced hardware problems. However, it has introduced patrons to user friendly access to information and has begun accustoming them to the use of new technology in libraries.

Some new journals and newsletters are being "published" or issued in electronic format or on disks. It is assumed that these will be acquired, if there is an expressed demand, from the materials or information resources budget.

Clearly, the same bits of information are becoming increasingly available in different media, at markedly different costs, and with different means of access.

Consequently, an emerging issue is how we will fund these new technological media. We are already strapped for funding for existing commitments. Resources are shrinking. We are faced with situations such as one database that is available online being equal in cost to several hard copy indexes that are more complete in nature.

Librarians must begin asking questions such as these:

1. How might these new technologies fit into the library's current omplement of microcomputers, online services, and related existing technologies and services?
.. Do any of the library's current suppliers produce or plan to produce and support these new products?
3. How many of the library's patrons are knowledgeable about and interested in access to information using the new media?
4. Can library staff participate in a hands-on pilot project to determine use and costs?
5. Can an appropriate budget for these new products be determined?
6. How should the library profession tackle common concerns and requirements related to these new formats?
7. How will librarians be involved in defining the "proper" use of the new formats for databases?

We might also ask:

1. How are they selected?
2. What long term effect will they have on the collection?
3. How will the addition of these new formats affect the more traditional acquisitions?
4. What will be the implications of libraries acquiring these new formats?

In considering the cost of purchasing these new formats, we must remember that they are workstation controlled. That is, each of these formats—whether CD-ROM, videodisc, or a database issued in the form of floppy discs—is dependent upon a specific type of workstation in order to access the stored information. These workstations vary in cost. Some of the media, such as InfoTrac's videodiscs, can be accessed from several connected workstations at the same time. Some require individual workstations.

Even when linking workstations, we are still limiting the number of users at a given time. We can expect a certain number of searches of the new format to take place in a defined time period. *But,* only one patron can use a workstation at a time. Thus, while increasing storage ability and easing access, we have also limited access to information. An example: if we acquire an encyclopedia on CD-ROM, one person can access that encyclopedia through a single workstation. In traditional hard copy format, the number of users of the encyclopedia at one time would be dictated by the number of volumes in the set. Similarly, *Books in Print* on CD-ROM is accessible by one person at one workstation while in hard copy the number of potential users at one time is determined by the number of volumes in this year's version of *BIP*.

Publishers view these new formats as ways to potentially increase revenue. Some libraries may be able to cancel hard copy subscriptions in favor of the new formats but most libraries will have to weigh the fact that the new storage media are workstation bound and thus the number of people who can use the service at one time is limited. Libraries that have subscribed to InfoTrac have found that they must limit the time that individual patrons can work at a station, for example.

We hope that publishers, recognizing that libraries cannot cancel hard copy versions of reference works in favor of the CD-ROM version, with limited access at a given time, will continue to produce the works in multiple formats. An advantage the library subscribing to new format reference works may find is that updates are more readily available for the new formats, are more convenient to use, and they are cumulated more quickly.

Online access to some reference databases may be cost effective in smaller libraries, and may enable the library to cancel some expensive hard copy subscriptions, but for larger libraries, with many patrons needing the same databases at the same time, the online access costs could be astronomical. A special library, serving a limited clientele, might be able to rely on databases accessed online. A large academic library, with its interdisciplinary clientele, will need the databases in hard copy as well as online.

For most libraries, the acquisition of information in these newer formats is supplementary to the acquisition of the same information in traditional forms. We acquire the new media for faster access, for the introduction of our patrons to the new technology, for the purpose of acclimating them to the new formats and to encourage the research process among reluctant students. While some databases, such as InfoTrac, may be limited in nature, its ease of use and attractiveness will at least get the undergraduate initiated into the research process—we hope. The library staff will have to expand the undergraduate's research techniques from that point.

The new technology enables us to access directly some large databases that formerly required mainframes so the new technology has freed us from the computer center and those accompanying overhead costs. With formerly mainframe-sized databases now accessible via microcomputer, access to information is possible for a larger group of users. Databases, formerly accessible only in large research centers, are now available on CD-ROM, or as in the case of one Bureau of the Census database, on 33 floppy diskettes. As more of us move into online catalogs with remote access, we can also explore mounting other databases on the mainframe, accessible via the online catalog terminals.

Potentially the new technology could also provide us with the mechanism for storing larger amounts of static information, such as long back runs of periodicals or reference sets, in a compact form. For these types of storage, the fact that the information is workstation-based and thus limited to one user at one workstation may not become an issue. However, we must consider whether it is reasonable to expend funds to replace existing holdings, already paid for, with the same holdings in a different form rather than buying new titles.

There has also been a concern that the new storage media will lead to a proliferation of workstations. InfoTrac, from Information Access Corporation, uses one type of workstation. Only IAC products can be operated on that particular workstation configuration. With CD-ROM, on the other hand, there is the potential of different CD-ROM databases, being operational on the same workstation.

The bottom line is still the question: What are the budgetary considerations?

At the present single copies of a database on CD-ROM or videodisc may be all a given library can afford. It will become increasingly possible to have multiple station access, as it has with InfoTrac, within a single site. Or manufacturers may become willing to sell additional copies of a database at a reduced cost to a library. Quantity discounts may resolve the access problems. Costs may come down as sales increase and libraries and manufacturers reach more knowledgeable experience levels. We have seen this happen with other technologies.

Still, the costs for the convenience of online systems, whether they be videodiscs, CD-ROM, floppies, or online to BRS, can strain a budget already stretched to meet current commitments. Libraries have a specific amount of money that they can expend for the acquisition of information resources for the library. Ongoing commitments must be funded before additional potential purchases can be identified. Once the money has been set aside for subscriptions and other continuations available in more traditional format, there may still be established commitments for the remaining funds, for example, approval plans.

How then can the library plan on funding the new information formats?

The library can conduct a pilot project with one or two alternative information formats, study patron use and the effectiveness of the format, and then make a decision on permanent acquisition. Still the acquisition of even the pilot project system may have to replace the acquisition of another item for the collection. Libraries that have considered or actually endured projects to reduce the total number of active periodical subscriptions in order to reduce expenditures or to make room for new subscriptions will cringe at the possibility of determining what to cancel in order to acquire one of these databases in one of the new formats.

The impact of new technology, and the accompanying pressure to acquire the new formats, on an already strained budget will be stressful. If the hardware costs can be separated from the acquisition of the media, which is advisable, then the ongoing cost will be for the database or reference work itself.

Even so, with our strained budgets, if the parent institution wishes the library to venture into the new information technology, that funding authority must be prepared to provide additional funding, either in the form of an increased budget or separate funding, earmarked for new means of information access. If the library initiates the acquisition of new information technology, it should justify additional funding for such acquisitions. Whichever funding course is pursued, eventually the funding should be consolidated into the information resources budget.

How much will it cost? At this point in the development of new information formats, that is largely an unknown. Just as with any other acquisition, the library will have to determine what is available, what subjects are covered and which fit the collection development needs of the library, what the costs will be, whether the hardware is affordable, and if the potential use of the new storage media will warrant the outlay of substantial funds for the media and the hardware. The number of databases available online has grown 20-30 percent a year in recent years. If the information available in these new formats grows at a comparable rate, the bottom line could be a substantial expenditure.

Is it worth it? Speed of access, exposure of patrons to new means of accessing information, and user friendliness will make it hard to resist the new formats. The potential use of the new media for storage of large bodies of information that normally receive low use will also make them very attractive from the viewpoint of preservation and space considerations.

However, the library staff must remember that just as library budgets have had to stretch to meet existing demands for books, periodicals, microformats, and binding, those same budgets will have to either pay for the new formats by dropping some present commitments, or additional funding must be acquired.

There are other budgetary considerations that libraries cannot afford to overlook when acquiring the new formats. One is how we will decide which of the new databases or reference works we will acquire in one of the new formats. Certainly we will use our collection development policy as a guideline but we will also have to evaluate the new format for its potential value to the collection. If the producer will let us use the service on an experimental basis for a short time in order to test its effectiveness and relevance to the collection, the decision will be easier to make. If this is not possible, we may have to make a decision based on comments from colleagues at other libraries or on observations at conferences.

Once the new format is in house, other costs will materialize: staff time to keep the system functioning properly; acquisition of supplies; staff time for instruction and advice on use of the new technology; potential acquisition of additional hardware; and environmental or housing considerations, such as additional electrical lines, improved lighting, or the purchase of appropriate furniture for the workstations.

Acquisition of new information formats for databases needed for internal library applications may be more easily accomplished and justified in terms of staff labor savings. If these new formats replace already acquired sets, the question of keeping or discarding library materials arises. Purchase of some databases for acquisitions or cataloging activities may substitute for other bibliographic services and the costs may be covered in that way.

For all of us in libraries with shrinking resources, and increased demands, the acquisition and maintenance of the new format — after the initial costs of the decision-making process—will not be an easy problem to resolve.

We are at a similar developmental stage as our predecessors were when microformats became common in libraries. We are just beginning to study the impact of the new technology on information access. We must realize that we will face potential resistance to these new storage formats as we have with microforms.

Before cancelling hard copy editions of resources, we must study use patterns to see if moving to a workstation bound media is feasible. We must consider several users needing access at a given time. There are also peripheral costs that will have to be absorbed: for hardware, for suppliers, or for space for the workstations.

It may be helpful to form a faculty Task Force to discuss how information is and will be available and how they, the faculty, access information for their research purposes.

While we are at the beginning of exploring these information access issues, we should not be hesitant to plunge in and assess costs and the impact on the collection. If we are hesitant, we may find some of our clientele acquiring information in the new formats on a departmental basis, thus eliminating the library's role in information access, or we may find the computer center assuming this role with their willingness to grow technologically.

REFERENCES

Ernest, Douglas J. and Monath, Jennifer. "User Reaction to a Computerized Periodical Index." *College and Research Library News*. 47:315-318, May 1986.

Fayen, Emily Gallup. "Beyond Technology: Rethinking 'Librarian'." *American Libraries*. 17:240-242, April 1986.

Griffith, Cary. "May the Source be with You." *Library Journal*. 112:55-57, February 1, 1987.

Helgerson, Linda W. "CD-ROM: A Revolution in the Making." *Library Hi Tech*. 4:23-27, Spring 1986.

———. "CD-ROM Search and Retrieval Software: The Requirements and Realities." *Library Hi Tech*, 4:69-77, Summer 1986.

Kuhlman, James R. and Lee, Everett S. "Data-Power to the People." *American Libraries*. 17:757-758, 760, 778, November 1986.

"Library Automation Update." *American Libraries*. 17:248-250, April 1986.

Miller, David C. "Laser Disks at the Library Door: The Microsoft First International Conference on CD-ROM." *Library Hi Tech*. 4:55-68, Summer 1986.

———. "Running with CD-ROM." *American Libraries*. 17:754-756.

Molholt, Pat. "The Information Machine: A New Challenge for Librarians." *Library Journal*. 111:47-52, October 1, 1986.

"Onward with Discs." *Library Journal*. 112:44, January 1987.

Poole, Jay Martin and St. Clair, Gloriana. "Funding Online Services from the Materials Budget." *College and Research Libraries*. 47:225-237, May 1986.

Roose, Tina. "The New Papyrus: CD-ROM in Your Library." *Library Journal.* 111:166-167, September 1, 1986.

Stephens, Kent. "Laserdisc Technology Enters Mainstream: Easy-to-Use Periodical Index Gets Heavy Use at California University." *American Libraries.* 17:252, April 1986.

Tenopir, Carol. "InfoTrac: a Laser Disc System." *Library Journal.* 111:168-169, September 1, 1986.

Van Arsdale, William O. "The Rush to Optical Discs." 111:53-55, October 1, 1986.

_____ and Ostrye, Anne T. "InfoTrac: A Second Opinion." *American Libraries.* 17:514-515, July/August 1986.

Williams, Martha E. "Highlights of the Online Database Field — Statistics, Pricing and New Delivery Mechanisms." *Proceedings of the Fifth National Online Meeting.* Medford, N.J.: Learned Information, 1984, p. 1.

Acquisitions, Budgets
and Materials Costs:
A Selected Bibliography

Lenore Clark

Although the problems of the eighties are in themselves not new to libraries, the dilemma confronting libraries today results from the confluence and intensification of these difficulties: more than fifteen years of escalating materials costs coupled with surging growth of information, increased user demands, a weakened dollar abroad, austere higher education budgets, and rapidly advancing technologies for information transfer. Librarians are grappling with questions of how to manage the acquisition of library materials in the face of dwindling purchasing power.

The theme of this bibliography centers on those concerns. Following the conference papers, topics are subdivided under the following headings: Approval Plans, The Impact and Management of Rising Materials Costs, Discriminatory Pricing and Acquisition of New Information Formats.

Readings have been selected for their authoritativeness and timeliness, and for their amplification of issues addressed in the papers.

APPROVAL PLANS

Since the late sixties approval plans have become an increasingly prominent method of monograph acquisition in libraries throughout the country. Critics and advocates alike acknowledge the major impact approval plans have had on acquisitions practices, on staffing, on materials budget allocation, and on collection development generally. As a result, a large, well defined literature has emerged: Books, conference papers, and articles address every aspect of approval plans. Two excellent annotated bibliographies on approval plans have been com-

Lenore Clark is Coordinator of Collection Development at the University of Oklahoma.

piled recently: Rossi's substantial "Library Approval Plans: A Selected, Annotated Bibliography," and Snoke and Loup's literature review in *Comparison of Approval Plan Profiles and Supplementary Collection Development Activities in Selected ARL Libraries*. McCullough's *Approval Plans and Academic Libraries* offers a solid retrospective bibliography beginning with the 1950s.

The following citations cover the most significant readings on approval plans since 1969:

Alessi, Dana. "Coping with Library Needs: The Approval Vendor's Response/Responsibility." In *Issues in Acquisitions: Programs & Evaluation*, edited by Sul H. Lee, pp. 91-109. Ann Arbor: Pierian Press, 1984.

Almagro, Bertha R. "Approval Plan: The Vendor Influence." Paper presented at the Joint Meeting of the Medical Library Group of Southern California and Arizona and North California and Nevada, held in Tucson, Arizona, at the Holiday Inn Broadway, February 20-22, 1985. Xerox.

"Approval and Gathering Plans." In *Melcher on Acquisitions*, by Daniel Melcher, pp. 109-16. Chicago: American Library Association, 1971.

Association of Research Libraries. Office of Management Studies. *Approval Plans in ARL Libraries*. Washington, D.C., 1982. (SPEC Kit no. 83).

Axford, H. William. "The Economics of a Domestic Approval Plan." *College & Research Libraries* 32 (September 1971):368-75.

Beck, Sara Ramser. "Librarian-Faculty Role in Collection Development with Approval Programs." In *Issues in Acquisitions: Programs & Evaluation*, edited by Sul H. Lee, pp. 55-68. Ann Arbor: Pierian Press, 1984.

Cargill, Jennifer, and Alley, Brian. "Highlights from a National Approval Plan Survey." *Technicalities* 1 (January 1981):3-5.

_____. *Practical Approval Plan Management*. Phoenix, AZ: Oryx Press, 1979.

DeVilbiss, Mary Lee. "The Approval-Built Collection in the Medium-Sized Academic Library." *College & Research Libraries* 36 (November 1975):487-92.

DeVolder, Arthur L. "Approval Plans — Bounty or Bedlam?" *Publishers Weekly* 202 (3 July 1972):18-20.

_____ "Why Continue on Approval Plan?" *Mountain-Plains Library Quarterly* (Summer 1972):11-16.

Dobbyn, Margaret. "Approval Plan Purchasing in Perspective." *College & Research Libraries* 33 (November 1972):480-84.

Duchin, Douglas. "The Jobber as a Surrogate Acquisitions Librarian." *Library Acquisitions: Practice and Theory* 7 (1983):17-20.

Dudley, Norman. "The Blanket Order." *Library Trends* 18 (January 1970):318-27.

Evans, G. Edward. "Book Selection and Book Collection Usage in Academic Libraries." *Library Quarterly* 40 (July 1970):297-308.

Evans, G. Edward, and Argyres, Claudia White. "Approval Plans and Collection Development in Academic Libraries." *Library Resources & Technical Services* 18 (Winter 1974):35-50.

Frye, Gloria, and Romanansky, Marcia. "The Approval Plan – The Core of an Academic Wholesaler's Business." In *Issues in Acquisitions: Programs & Evaluation*, edited by Sul H. Lee, pp. 111-19. Ann Arbor: Pierian Press, 1984.

Grant, Joan, and Perlmuter, Susan. "Vendor Performance Evaluation." *Journal of Academic Librarianship* 4 (November 1978):366-67.

Gregor, Jan, and Fraser, Wendy Carol. "A University of Windsor Experience with an Approval Plan in Three Subjects and Three Vendors." *Canadian Library Journal* 38 (August 1981):227-31.

Hodge, Stanley P. "Evaluating the Role and Effectiveness of Approval Plans for Library Collection Development." In *Issues in Acquisitions: Programs & Evaluation*, edited by Sul H. Lee, pp. 33-53. Ann Arbor: Pierian Press, 1984.

Hulbert, Linda Ann, and Curry, David Stewart. "Evaluation of an Approval Plan." *College & Research Libraries* 39 (November 1978):485-91.

Kautz, B. A. "Approval Plans: A Time Saver for Agriculture Bibliographers." *International Association of Agricultural Librarians and Documentalists Quarterly Bulletin* 30 (1985):1-6.

Kevil, L. Hunter. "The Approval Plan of Smaller Scope." *Library Acquisitions: Practice and Theory* 9 (1985):13-20.

Loe, Mary H. "Thor Tax Ruling After 5 Years: Its Effect on Publishing and Libraries." *Library Acquisitions: Practice and Theory* 10 (1986):203-18.

McCullough, Kathleen. "Approval Plans: Vendor Responsibility and Library Research, a Literature Survey and Discussion." *College & Research Libraries* 33 (September 1972):368-81.

McCullough, Kathleen; Posey, Edwin D.; and Pickett, Doyle C. *Approval Plans and Academic Libraries: An Interpretive Survey*. Phoenix, AZ: Oryx Press, 1977.

McDonald, David R.; Maxfield, Margaret W.; and Friesner, Virginia G.F. "Sequential Analysis: A Methodology for Monitoring Approval Plans." *College & Research Libraries* 40 (July 1979):329-34.

Mann, Sallie E. "Approval Plans as a Method of Collection Development." *North Carolina Libraries* 43 (Spring 1985):12-14.

Meyer, Betty J., and Demos, John T. "Acquisitions Policy for University Libraries: Selection or Collection." *Library Resources & Technical Services* 14 (Summer 1970):395-99.

Morrison, Perry D.; Merritt, LeRoy C.; Browne, Joseph P.; and Shepard, Stanley A. "A Symposium on Approval Order Plans and the Book Selection Responsibilities of Librarians." *Library Resources & Technical Services* 12 (Spring 1968):133-45.

Myrick, William J., Jr. "The Use of Approval Plans by Large Academic Libraries in Times of Fiscal Stringency: A Brief Report." *Library Acquisitions: Practice and Theory* 1 (1977):83-87.

Newborn, Dennis E., and Godden, Irene P. "Improving Approval Plan Performance: A Case Study." *Library Acquisitions: Practice and Theory* 4 (1980):145-55.

Perrault, Anne H. "A New Dimension in Approval Plan Service." *Library Acquisitions: Practice and Theory* 7 (1983):35-40.

Posey, Edwin D., and McCullough, Kathleen. "Approval Plans One Year Later: The Purdue Experience with Separate School Plans." In *New Horizons for Academic Libraries: Papers Presented at the First National Conference of the Association of Colleges and Research Libraries, Boston, Massachusetts, November 8-11, 1978*, edited by Robert D. Stueart and Richard D. Johnson, pp. 483-89. New York: K. G. Saur, 1979.

Rebuldela, Harriet K. "Some Administrative Aspects of Blanket Ordering: A Response." *Library Resources & Technical Services* 13 (Summer 1969):342-45.

Reidelbach, John H., and Shirk, Gary M. "Selecting an Approval Plan Vendor: A Step-by-Step Process." *Library Acquisitions: Practice and Theory* 7 (1983):115-22.

_____. "Selecting an Approval Plan Vendor II: Comparative Vendor Data." *Library Acquisitions: Practice and Theory* 8 (1984):157-202.

_____. "Selecting an Approval Plan Vendor III: Academic Librarians' Evaluations of Eight United States Approval Plan Vendors." *Library Acquisitions: Practice and Theory* 9 (1985):177-260.

Rossi, Gary J. "Library Approval Plans: A Selected Annotated Bibliography." *Library Acquisitions: Practice and Theory* 11 (1987):3-34.

Rouse, Roscoe. "Automation Stops Here: A Case for Man-Made Book Collections." *College & Research Libraries* 31 (May 1970): 147-54.

Schmidt, Karen A. "Capturing the Mainstream: Publisher-Based and Subject-Based Approval Plans in Academic Libraries." *College & Research Libraries* 47 (July 1986):365-69.

Shirk, Gary M. "Evaluating Approval Plan Vendor Performance: Toward a Rationale and Model." In *Issues in Acquisitions: Programs & Evaluation*, edited by Sul H. Lee, pp. 11-31. Ann Arbor: Pierian Press, 1984.

Snoke, Helen Lloyd, and Loup, Jean L. *Comparison of Approval Plan Profiles and Supplementary Collection Development Activities in Selected ARL Libraries: A Report to the Council on Library Resources*. November 1986 (forthcoming in ERIC).

Spyers-Duran, Peter. "Approval Plans, Publishers, and the Supreme Court." *Technicalities* 1 (March 1981):12.

Spyers-Duran, Peter, ed. *Approval and Gathering Plans in Academic Libraries: Proceedings of the International Seminar on Approval and Gathering Plans in Large and Medium Size Academic Libraries Held at Western Michigan University, November 14, 1968*. Littleton, CO: Libraries Unlimited, 1969.

Spyers-Duran, Peter, and Gore, Daniel, eds. *Advances in Understanding Approval and Gathering Plans in Academic Libraries: International Seminar on Approval and Gathering Plans in Large and Medium Size Academic Libraries, second, Western Michigan University, 1969*. Kalamazoo: Western Michigan University, 1970.

_____. *Economics of Approval Plans: Proceedings of the Third International Seminar on Approval and Gathering Plans in Large and Medium Size Academic Libraries, held in the Ramada Inn, West Palm Beach, Florida, February 17-19, 1971*. Westport, CT: Greenwood Press, 1972.

Spyers-Duran, Peter, and Mann, Thomas Jr., eds. *Shaping Library Collections for the 1980s*. Phoenix, AZ: Oryx Press, 1980.

Stave, Don. "Art Books on Approval: Why Not?" *Library Acquisitions: Practice and Theory* 7 (1983):12-14.

Steele, Colin. "Blanket Orders and the Bibliographer in the Large Research Library." *Journal of Librarianship* 2 (October 1970): 272-80.

Stueart, Robert D. "Mass Buying Programs in the Development Process." In *Collection Development in Libraries: A Treatise*, edited by Robert D. Stueart, and George B. Miller, Jr., pp. 203-17. Greenwich, CT: Jai Press, 1979.

Taggart, W. R. "Blanket Approval Ordering—A Positive Approach." *Canadian Library Journal* 21 (July-August 1970):286-89.

_____. "The Pros & Cons of Blanket Approval Book Acquisitions Plans." *CACUL Newsletter* 3 (February 1972):165-71.

Thom, Ian W. "Some Administrative Aspects of Blanket Ordering." *Library Resources & Technical Services* 13 (Summer 1969):338-42.

_____. "Some Administrative Aspects of Blanket Ordering: Rejoinder to a Response." *Library Resources & Technical Services* 13 (Summer 1969):345-46.

"Vendor-Controlled Order Plans." In *Acquisitions Management and Collection Development in Libraries*, by Magrill, Rose Mary, and Hickey, Doralyn, pp. 95-109. Chicago: American Library Association, 1984.

Walters, Mary D. "Approval Program Timing Study: Baker & Taylor vs. Blackwell North America." *Collection Building* 7 (Spring 1985):14-18.

Wilden-Hart, Marion. "Long-Term Effects of Approval Plans." *Library Resources & Technical Services* 14 (Summer 1970):400-406.

RISING MATERIALS COSTS:
IMPACT AND MANAGEMENT

Faced on the one hand with rising costs and, on the other, with leaner budgets and expanding user demands, libraries are resorting to a variety of strategies to maintain effective acquisitions, from increased fund-raising efforts, greater management efficiencies, and stepped-up communication with publishers, to cancellation of serials.

The following references focus on the description and documentation of materials price increases, their impact on libraries acquisitions practices, and libraries' responses to the stresses of eroding buying power. The emphasis is on the cost side of materials management rather than internal allocation. Items marked with asterisks represent regularly published reports on prices which serve to trace the rise in materials costs over the years. Only the most recent issues are listed.

Almagro, Bertha R. "Budgeting and Planning: A Tandem Approach." *Serials Librarian* 10 (Fall 1985/Winter 1985-86):173-79.

Anderson, David C. "Journals for Academic Veterinary Libraries: Price Increases, 1977 and 1983 Through 1986." *Serials Librarian* 11 (October 1986):41-49.

Association of Research Libraries. Office of Management Studies. *Cost Studies and Fiscal Planning*. Washington, D.C., 1979. (SPEC Kit no. 52.)

Association of Research Libraries. Office of Management Studies. *Determining Indirect Cost Rates in Research Libraries*. Washington, D.C., 1977. (SPEC Kit no. 34.)

Association of Research Libraries. Office of Management Studies. *Indirect Cost Rates in Research Libraries*. Washington, D.C., 1980. (SPEC Kit no. 64.)

Association of Research Libraries. Office of Management Studies. *Library Materials Cost Studies*. Washington, D.C., 1980. (SPEC Kit no. 60.)

Association of Research Libraries. Office of Management Studies. *Library Materials Cost Studies in ARL Libraries*. Washington, D.C., 1983. (SPEC Kit no. 95.)

Association of Research Libraries. Office of Management Studies. *Preparation and Presentation of the Library Budget*. Washington, D.C., 1977. (SPEC Kit no. 32.)

Axford, H. William. "The Validity of Book Price Indexes for Budgeting Projections." *Library Resources & Technical Services* 19 (Winter 1975):5-12.

Barschall, Henry H. "The Cost of Physics Journals." *Physics Today* 39 (December 1986):34-36.

Bellanger, Charles H., and Lavellee, Lise. "Towards a Periodical and Monograph Price Index." *College and Research Libraries* 42 (September 1981):416-24.

Bonk, Sharon C. "Rethinking the Acquisitions Budget: Anticipating and Managing Change." *Library Acquisitions: Practice and Theory* 10 (1986):97-106.

Boswood, Michael. "The Future of Serials, 1976-2000: A Publisher's Perspective." *Serials Librarian* 11 (December 1986/January 1987):9-17.

Clack, Mary E., and Williams, Sally F. "Using Locally and Nationally Produced Periodical Price Indexes in Budget Preparation." *Library Resources & Technical Services* 27 (October/December 1983):346-56.

Cross, Nigel. "The Economics of Learned Journal Publishing." *Times Literary Supplement* 23 November 1984, p. 1348.

Cunningham, George. "The Upward Creep in Book Prices Before

Publication." *Library Association Record* 87 (November 1985): 439.

Curtis, Mary E. "Financial Management in Publishing Journals." *Scholarly Publishing* 17 (October 1985):65-72.

DeGennaro, Richard. "Escalating Journal Prices: Time to Fight Back." *American Libraries* 8 (February 1977):69-74.

"Dollar's Fall Causes Cutbacks in Purchase of Foreign Pubns." *Library Journal* 112 (May 1987):18.

Dougherty, Richard M. "Discrimination, Devaluation, and Exploitation: The Library and Campus Dilemma." Presented to University of Michigan Senate Assembly, 16 February 1987. Xerox and slides.

_____. "Journal Subscription Pricing: What's in Store for 1987?" *Library Issues* 7 (January 1987):4.

_____. "The Scoreboard: Differential Pricing of Periodical Subscriptions." *Library Issues* 6 (March 1986):2.

_____ "The Scoreboard: Differential Pricing of Periodical Subscriptions." *Library Issues* 6 (March 1986):2.

_____ "The Scoreboard: Differential Pricing of Periodical Subscriptions—Continued." *Library Issues* 6 (July 1986):4.

Dove, Paul H. "Subscription Costs: A Five Year Comparison." *South Carolina Librarian* 28 (Spring 1984):9-11.

Emery, Charles D. "Forecasting Models and the Prediction of Periodical Subscription Costs." *Serials Librarian* 9 (Summer 1985):5-22.

"European Mathematical Council Survey of European Mathematical Periodicals." *Notices of the American Mathematical Society* 33 (November 1986):905-9.

Fast, Barry. "Publishing & Bookselling: A Look at Some Idiosyncracies." *Library Acquisitions: Practice and Theory* 3 (1979):15-17.

Fry, Bernard M., and White, Herbert S. "Impact of Economic Pressures on American Libraries and Their Decision Concerning Scholarly and Research Journal Acquisitions & Retention." *Library Acquisitions: Practice & Theory* 3 (1979):153-237.

*Grannis, Chandler B. "1986: The Year in Review; Title Output Level, Prices Stabilized." *Publishers Weekly* 231 (March 1987):16-19.

*_____. "U.S. Book Title Output and Average Prices, 1983-1985." *Publishers Weekly* 230 (October 1986):89-92.

Greene, Philip E. N., III. "Serials Prices: An Historical Perspective." *Serials Librarian* 11 (December 1986/January 1987):19-29.

Hale, Charles E. "Library Consumerism: A Need for Concerted Action." *Technicalities* 4 (May 1984):8-9.

Harvey, John F., and Spyers-Duran, Peter. "The Effect of Inflation on Academic Libraries." In *Austerity Management in Academic Libraries*, edited by John F. Harvey and Peter Spyers-Duran, pp. 1-42. Metuchen, NJ: Scarecrow Press, 1984.

Hurst, Christopher. "The Pricing Merry-Go-Round." *The Bookseller* 4233 (February 1987):473-74.

Jones, Graham. "The Price and the Package: Your Library Press." *Library Review* 35 (Autumn 1986):188-90.

*Knapp, Leslie C., and Lenzini, Rebecca T. "Price Index for 1987: U.S. Periodicals." *Library Journal* 112 (April 1987):39-44.

Kronenfeld, Michael R., and Thompson, James A. "The Impact of Inflation on Journal Costs." *Library Journal* 106 (April 1981):714-17.

*Leach, Ronald G. "Library Materials Price Update." *Library Issues* 7 (January 1987):2-3.

*Lenzini, Rebecca T. "Periodical Prices 1984-1986 Update." *Serials Librarian* 11 (September 1986):107-15.

Lee, Sul H., ed. *Pricing and Costs of Monographs and Serials: National and International Issues*. (*Journal of Library Administration* Supplement no. 1), Fall 1986.

"The Library Dollar." *Australian Academic and Research Libraries* 10 (June 1979):99-104.

Lynden, Frederick. "Financial Planning for Collection Management." *Journal of Library Administration* 3 (Fall/Winter 1982): 109-20.

_____. "Library Materials Budgeting in the Private University Library: Austerity and Action." In *Advances in Librarianship*, vol. 10, edited by Michael H. Harris, pp. 89-154. New York: Academic Press, 1980.

_____. "Library Materials Cost Studies." *Library Resources & Technical Services* 27 (April/June 1983):156-62.

_____. "Sources of Information on the Costs of Library Materials." *Library Acquisitions: Practice and Theory* 1 (1977):105-16.

Nitecki, Danuta. "An Attitudinal Problem." (Academic Libraries, Online Searching, and Turf: A Symposium) *Journal of Academic Librarianship* 11 (November 1985):274.

Page, Gillian. "Economics of Journal Publishing: The Publisher's Viewpoint." In *Economics of Serials Management: Proceedings of the Second Blackwell's Periodicals Conference, held at Trinity College, Oxford, 23-24 March 1977*, edited by David P. Woodworth, pp. 52-71. Loughborough, England: Serials Group, n.d.

Paul, Huibert. "Serials: Higher Prices vs. Shrinking Budgets." *Serials Librarian* 9 (Winter 1984):3-12.

Pearson, Lois R. "Falling Dollar Imperils Research Collections." *American Libraries* 18 (May 1987):317-18.

*"Periodical Prices." *Library Association Record* 88 (May 1986):255-56.

Sabosik, Patricia E. "Editorial: 1986 College Book Prices." *Choice* 24 (March 1987):1005.

Sampson, Gary S. "Allocating the Book Budget: Measuring for Inflation." *College and Research Libraries* 39 (September 1978):381-83.

*Sandler, Mark. "Dollar Watch: Fourth Quarter Update." *Library Issues* 7 (March 1987):3.

Smith, Dennis. "Forecasting Price Increase Needs for Library Materials: The University of California Experience." *Library Resources & Technical Services* 28 (April/June 1984):136-48.

*Soupiset, Kathryn A. "College Book Price Information, 1986." *Choice* 24 (March 1987):1006-1010.

"Survey of American Research Journals." *Notices of the American Mathematical Society* 33 (March 1986):287-91.

Taylor, David C. "The High Cost of Serials." In *Issues in Library Management: A Reader for the Professional Librarian*, pp. 64-81. White Plains, NY: Knowledge Industry, 1984.

_____. "The Love-Hate Relationship of Librarians and Publishers of Serials." *Drexel Library Quarterly* 21 (Winter 1985):29-36.

Tuttle, Marcia. "The Serials Manager's Obligation." *Library Resources & Technical Services* 31 (April/June 1987):135-47.

Varma, D. K. "Increasing Subscription Costs and Problems of Resource Allocation." *Special Libraries* 74 (January 1983):61-66.

Walch, David B. "Budgeting for Non-Print Media in Academic Libraries." In *New Horizons for Academic Libraries: Papers Presented at the First National Conference of the Association of College and Research Libraries, Boston, Massachusetts, November 8-11, 1978*, edited by Robert D. Stueart and Richard D. Johnson, pp. 341-51. New York: K. G. Saur, 1979.

_____. "Price Index for Nonprint Media." *Library Journal* 106 (February 1981):432-3.

Waltner, Nellie L.; King, Cyrus B.; and Horner, William C. "Periodical Prices: A Comparison of Local and National Averages." *Library Acquisitions: Practice and Theory* 1 (1977):237-41.

Welsh, Erwin K. "European Collection Development in American Libraries: Problems and Prospects." In *Acquisition of Foreign Ma-*

terials for U.S. Libraries, 2d ed., edited by Theodore Samore, pp. 125-41. Metuchen, NJ: Scarecrow Press, 1982.

White, Herbert S. "Budgetary Priorities in the Administration of Large Academic Libraries." In *New Horizons for Academic Libraries: Papers Presented at the First National Conference of the Association of College and Research Libraries, Boston, Massachusetts, November 8-11, 1978*, edited by Robert D. Stueart and Richard D. Johnson, pp. 352-56. New York: K.G. Saur, 1979.

_____. "Library Materials Prices and Academic Library Practices: Between Scylla and Charybdis." *Journal of Academic Librarianship* 5 (March 1979):20-23.

_____. "Publishers, Libraries, and Costs of Journal Subscriptions in Times of Funding Retrenchment." *Library Quarterly* 46 (October 1976):359-77.

_____. "Strategies and Alternatives in Dealing with the Serials Management Budget." In *Serials Collection Development: Choices and Strategies*, edited by Sul H. Lee, pp. 27-42. Ann Arbor: Pierian Press, 1981.

White, Herbert S., and Fry, Bernard M. "Economic Interaction Between Special Libraries and Publishers of Scholarly and Research Journals: Results of an NSF Study." *Special Libraries* 68 (March 1977):109-14.

Williams, Sally F. "Budget Justification: Closing the Gap between Request and Result." *Library Resources & Technical Services* 28 (April/June 1984):129-35.

_____. "Construction and Application of a Periodical Price Index." *Collection Management* 2 (Winter 1978):329-44.

*Wood, Lawraine. *Average Prices of British Academic Books: 1974-1984 (Report/CLAIM, no. 41)*. Loughborough: Centre for Library and Information Management, Department of Library and Information Studies, 1984.

_____. "University Monograph Acquisition and the Sterling Exchange Rate." *Outlook on Research Libraries* 7 (August 1985):8-10.

DISCRIMINATORY PRICING

Not since the twenties and thirties has discriminatory pricing been so conspicuous a concern in library acquisitions. Straightened by continuing inflation and institutional austerity, libraries are reacting to exorbitant prices in an increasingly consumerist manner. A substantial body of literature has emerged around the issue, comprised principally of documented price comparisons, discussions of pricing policies, declarations of concern, and publicized actions of individual libraries.

To provide historical perspective, this section includes, in addition to recent literature, a selection of readings from the 1920s and 1930s, when a similar form of discriminatory pricing agitated the library community.

"ARL Statement on Discriminatory Journal Pricing." *Association of Research Libraries Newsletter* 135. (June 18, 1986):4.

Astle, Deana, and Hamaker, Charles. "Pricing by Geography: British Journal Pricing 1986, Including Developments in Other Countries." *Library Acquisitions: Practice and Theory* 10 (1986):165-81.

Besant, Larry X., and Ruschin, Siegfried. "Price of European Journals." *Nature* 310 (August 1984):358.

Boissonnas, Christian M. "Differential Pricing of Monographs and Serials." Condensed by Nancy E. Barr. *Library Issues* 7 (November 1986):1-2.

Bullard, Scott R. "A Report of the RTSD RS Bookdealer-Library Relations Committee Open Meeting, June 26, 1984." *Library Acquisitions: Practice and Theory* 8 (1984):259-60.

_____. "Highlights of the Bookdealer/Library Relations Committee: or, For Starters, Don't Call Her Company 'Mister'." *Library Acquisitions: Practice and Theory* 10 (1986):281-82.

Courtney, Keith. "British Journal Pricing: A Publisher's View." *Serials Librarian* 11 (December 1986/January 1987):163-65.

Dorn, Knut, and Maddox, Jane. "The Acquisition of European Journals." *Library Acquisitions: Practice and Theory* 10 (1986):199-202.

Dougherty, Richard M. "Editorial: Combatting Differential Pricing of Journals." *Journal of Academic Librarianship* 11 (November 1985):267.

Dyl, Edward A. "A Note on Price Discrimination by Academic Journals." *Library Quarterly* 53 (May 1983):161-68.

"Foreign Journal Prices." *Association of Research Libraries Newsletter* 126 (26 July 1985):3.

"Foreign Journal Vendors and Price Gouging." *Library Journal* 109 (March 1984):411.

Hamaker, Charles. "Journal Pricing: A Modest Proposal." *Serials Librarian* 11 (December 1986/January 1987):171-75.

Hamaker, Charles, and Astle, Deana A. "Recent Pricing Patterns in

British Journal Publishing." *Library Acquisitions: Practice and Theory* 8 (1984):225-32.

Houbeck, Robert L., Jr. "British Journal Pricing: Enigma Variations, or What *Will* the U.S. Market Bear?" *Library Acquisitions: Practice and Theory* 10 (1986):183-97.

Joyce, Patrick, and Merz, Thomas E. "Price Discrimination in Academic Journals." *Library Quarterly* 55 (July 1985):273-83.

Learned Journals Pricing and Buying Round at Institution of Mechanical Engineers, Birdcage Walk, London SW 1 on Friday 22nd March 1985. Association of Learned and Professional Society Publishers and The Publishers Association. Letchworth, Herts, England: Epsilon Press, 1985.

Maddox, Jane. "Harrassowitz: A Detailed Response to VCH." *Library Acquisitions: Practice and Theory* 11 (1987):91-94.

Merriman, John. "British Journal Pricing: The Subscription Agent's View." *Serials Librarian* 11 (December 1986/January 1987):167-69.

Ruschin, Siegfried. "Why Are Foreign Subscription Rates Higher for American Libraries Than They Are for Subscribers Elsewhere?" *Serials Librarian* 9 (Spring 1985):7-17.

Tuttle, Marcia. "Discriminatory Pricing of British Scholarly Journals for the North American Market: An Overview." *Serials Librarian* 11 (December 1986/January 1987):157-61.

———. "North American Prices for British Scholarly Journals." *Library Acquisitions: Practice and Theory* 10 (1986):89-96.

———. "The Pricing of British Journals for the North American Market." *Library Resources & Technical Sources* 30 (January/March 1986):72-78.

White, Herbert S. "Differential Pricing." *Library Journal* 111 (September 1986):170-71.

"The Willet-Phelan Letters." *Library Acquisitions: Practice and Theory* 9 (1985):169-76.

Historical Readings

"Authentic Translation of Reply of Deutscher Verlegerverein to Resolution of the Medical Library Association Protesting Against the High Prices of German Medical Publications" and "Reply of Medical Library Association to German Publishers Regarding German Medical Publications." *Medical Library Association Bulletin*, new series 14 (1924):39-42.

Bonser, Wilfrid. "The Cost of German Periodicals." *Library Association Record* series 3, 3 (May 1933):162-63.
"Proclamation." *Medical Library Association Bulletin* 22 (November 1933):103-105.
"Report of Committee on Resolution Protesting Against High Prices of German Medical Books and Periodicals." *Medical Library Association Bulletin*, new series 15(1925):23-27.
"Report of the Committee on the Cost of Current Medical Periodicals." *Medical Library Association Bulletin* 22 (August 1933):9-12.
"Reports of Special Committees: Cost of German Periodicals." *Medical Library Association Bulletin* 25 (September 1935):38-51.

ACQUISITION OF NEW INFORMATION FORMATS

Rapidly advancing technologies have expanded the scope and flexibility of both bibliographic and textual access to information worldwide, extending "the principle of the bibliography from the level of reference to the level of collection. They have thereby introduced a means of organizing information previously achieved only through much effort. While members of the public continue to choose judiciously what books and periodicals to purchase or borrow from their libraries—extended by cumbersome interlibrary loans—those with the resources have ready access both to full-text databases and to yet a further level of information . . . " (Lorimer, p. 99) How, with budgets already badly strained, can libraries acquire new and costly information formats, and what should their relationship be to the conventional materials of acquisition?

The following references focus on funding implications of acquiring new information formats. Although technical processing and public service considerations are frequently inextricable from acquisition and collection of electronically transmitted knowledge, these readings are selected for their relevance to electronic information as resource rather than as service or system; that is, materials acquired for the library's collection.

"AL Automation Symposium: Will Optical Discs be the End of On-line Networks?" *American Libraries* 18 (April 1987):253-56.
Atkinson, Hugh. "Academic Librarians Respond: Can Technology Triumph Over Budgets." *Collection Building* 8 (1987):18-19.
Bartenbach, Bill. "CD-ROM and Libraries: Opportunities, Concerns,

Challenges." In *National Online Meeting Proceedings – 1987, New York, May 5-7, 1987*. Compiled by Martha E. Williams and Thomas H. Hogan, pp. 9-19, Medford, NJ: Learned Information, 1987.

Baumol, William J., and Blackman, Sue Anne Batey. "Electronics, the Cost Disease, and the Operation of Libraries." *Journal of the American Society for Information Science* 34 (May 1983):181-91.

Beltran, Ann Bristow. "Funding Computer-Assisted Reference in Academic Research Libraries." *Journal of Academic Librarianship* 13 (March 1987):4-7.

Butler, Matilda; Paisley, William; and Spigai, Frances. "CD ROM in the Matrix of Publishing Choices." In *CD ROM: The New Papyrus, the Current and Future State of the Art*, edited by Steve Lambert and Suzanne Ropiequet, pp. 453-66. Redmond, WA: Microsoft Press, 1986.

Chessen, James. "Economic Outlook." In *Online Searching: The Basics, Settings, and Management*, edited by Joann H. Lee, pp. 70-80. Littleton, CO: Libraries Unlimited, 1984.

Chiang, Katharine S. "Computer Accessible Material in the Academic Library: Avoiding the Kludge." In *Energies for Transition: Proceedings of the Fourth National Conference of the Association of College and Research Libraries, Baltimore, Maryland, April 9-12, 1986*, edited by Danuta A. Nitecki, pp. 67-69. Chicago: Association of College and Research Libraries, 1986.

Cogswell, James A. "On-Line Search Services: Implications for Libraries and Library Users." *College and Research Libraries* 39 (July 1978):275-80.

DeGennaro, Richard. "Impact of On-Line Services on the Academic Library." In *The On-Line Revolution in Libraries: Proceedings of the 1977 Conference in Pittsburgh, Pennsylvania*, edited by Allen Kent and Thomas J. Galvin, pp. 177-81. New York: Marcel Dekker, 1978.

_____. "Shifting Gears: Information Technology & the Academic Library." *Library Journal* 109 (June 15, 1984):1204-9.

Dowd, Sheila, Whaley, John H., and Pankake, Marcia. "Reactions to 'Funding Online Services from the Materials Budget.'" *College & Research Libraries* 47 (May 1986):230-37.

"Electronic Technology and Serials Publishing." *Library Systems Newsletter* 6 (November 1986):81-84.

Evans, John Edward. "Methods of Funding." In *Online Searching Technique and Management*, edited by James J. Maloney, pp. 135-48. Chicago: American Library Association, 1983.

Galloway, Margaret E., Lavender, Kenneth, Mitchell, George, and Floyd, William. "The Expanding Universe of Special Formats." *College & Research Libraries News* 47 (November 1986):650-54.

Griffith, Cary. "May the Source Be with You!" *Library Journal* 112 (February 1987):55-57.

Grimes, Nancy E. "Costs, Budgets, and Financial Management." In *Online Searching Technique and Management*, edited by James J. Maloney, pp. 123-34. Chicago: American Library Association, 1983.

Kantor, Paul B. "The Relation Between Costs and Services at Academic Libraries." In *Financing Information Services: Problems, Changing Approaches, and New Opportunities for Academic and Research Libraries*, edited by Peter Spyers-Duran and Thomas W. Mann, Jr., pp. 69-78. Westport, CT: Greenwood Press, 1985.

Kranich, Nancy C. "Find the Right Criteria, Then Decide About Fees." *Collection Building* 8 (1987):21-22.

Lancaster, F. Wilfrid, and Goldhor, Herbert. "The Impact of Online Services on Subscriptions to Printed Publications." *Online Review* 5 (August 1981):301-11.

"Libraries and Technology." In *Libraries and Librarians in an Age of Electronics*, by F. Wilfrid Lancaster, pp. 89-108. Arlington, VA: Information Resources Press, 1982.

Lorimer, Rowland. "Implications of the New Technologies of Information." *Scholarly Publishing* 16 (April 1985):197-210.

Magnuson, Barbara. "Collection Management: New Technology, New Decisions." *Wilson Library Bulletin* 57 (May 1983):736-41.

Martin, Murray S. "Financial Planning: New Needs, New Sources, New Styles." In *Financing Information Services: Problems, Changing Approaches and New Opportunities for Academic and Research Libraries*, edited by Peter Spyers-Duran and Thomas W. Mann, Jr., pp. 91-108. Westport, CT: Greenwood Press, 1985.

———. "The Organizational and Budgetary Effects of Automation on Libraries." In *Advances in Library Administration and Organization*, Vol. 2, pp. 69-83. Greenwich, CT: Jai Press, 1982.

Martin, Susan K. "More About Electronic Publishing: The Role of the Academic Library." *Library Issues* 3 (July 1983):4.

Melin, Nancy. "The New Alexandria: CD ROM in the Library." In *CD ROM: The New Papyrus, the Current and Future State of the Art*, edited by Steve Lambert and Suzanne Ropiequet, pp. 509-16. Redmond, WA: Microsoft Press, 1986.

"The Migration from Print on Paper." In *Libraries and Librarians in an Age of Electronics*, by F. Wilfrid Lancaster, pp. 109-23. Arlington, VA: Information Resources Press, 1982.

Miller, David C. "Running with CD-ROM." *American Libraries* 17 (November 1986):754-56.

Molholt, Pat, and Hohenberg, Paul M. "What Price the Information Age." Paper prepared for the Fourth Symposium on Empirical Foundation of Information and Software Sciences, Georgia Institute of Technology School of Information and Computer Science, Atlanta, Georgia, October 1986. Xerox.

Neely, Glanda. "Online Databases: Efforts on Reference Acquisitions." *Library Acquisitions: Practice and Theory* 5 (1981):45-49.

Pasqualini, Bernard F. *Dollars and Sense: Implications of the New Online Technology for Managing the Library. Proceedings of a Conference Program held in New York City, June 29, 1986. Machine-Assisted Reference Service Section, Reference and Adult Services Division, American Library Association*. Chicago: American Library Association, 1987.

"Planning for Libraries in Transition." In *The Economics of Research Libraries*, by Martin M. Cummings, pp. 96-122. Washington, D.C.: Council on Library Resources, 1986.

Poole, Jay Martin, and St. Clair, Gloriana. "Funding Online Services from the Materials Budget." *College & Research Libraries* 47 (May 1986):225-29.

Raitt, D. I. "Electronic Publishing—a View from the Library." *Electronic Publishing Review* 5 (September 1985):199-210.

Rochell, Carlton. "The Knowledge Business: Economic Issues of Access to Bibliographic Information." *College & Research Libraries* 46 (January 1985):5-12.

Roose, Tina. "The New Papyrus: CD-ROM in Your Library?" *Library Journal* 111 (September 1986):166-67.

Tenopir, Carol. "Change or Crisis in the Database Industry." *Library Journal* 111 (April 1986):46-47.

Turock, Betty J. "Technology and the Post-Industrial Society: The Academic Library in the 1980s and Beyond." *Catholic Library World* 55 (February 1984):298-304.

Turoff, Murray, and Hiltz, Starr Roxanne. "The Electronic Journal: A Progress Report." *Journal of the American Society for Information Science* 33 (July 1982):195-202.

Unruh, Betty. "Online Reference . . . No Longer an Option." *Reference Librarian* 5/6 (Fall/Winter 1982):83-91.

Van Arsdale, William O. "The Rush to Optical Discs." *Library Journal* 111 (October 1986):53-55.

Van Arsdale, William O., and Ostrye, Anne T. "Info Trac: A Second Opinion." *American Libraries* 17 (July/August 1986):514-15.

Walters, Edward M. "Electronic Journals and the Concept of a Paperless Library." *National Forum* 60:33-35.

Waters, Richard L., and Kralisz, Victor Frank. "Financing the Electronic Library: Models and Options." *Drexel Library Quarterly* 17 (Fall 1981):107-20.

Weiskel, Timothy C. "Libraries as Life-Systems: Information, Entropy, and Coevolution on Campus." *College & Research Libraries* 47 (November 1986):545-63.

Whitaker, Rebecca. "The Impact of Online Search Services on Libraries." In *Online Searching Technique and Management*, edited by James J. Maloney, pp. 166-72. Chicago: American Library Association, 1983.

Williams, Martha E. "Highlights of the Online Database Field — Statistics, Pricing and New Delivery Mechanisms." In *Proceedings of the Fifth National Online Meeting*, pp. 1-4. Medford, NJ: Learned Information, 1984.

Index

Ruschin, Siegfried 115

School Library Journal 71
Schrift, Leonard 58
Science 73
Seattle Pacific University 128
Seattle University 128
Serial prices
  Library Journal 121
  Michigan Study 108-110
Serials Librarian 99
SPEC Kit
  Approval plans 5
  Local cost studies 119
  #83 7
St. Clair, Gloriana 136
St. Martin's College 128
Stanford University 118
Supreme Court, U.S. 95

Tariff 95
Thor Power Tool Decision 58,76,95
Touzot 38
Tuttle, Marcia 96

UTLAS 6,7
University of Michigan 100,103,104,109
University of North Carolina 127
University of Puget Sound 128
University of Texas 49
University of Utah 6
University press 8,53,58

Van Nostrand 76
Verlag Chemie Publishing 115
Videodisc 136,138
Vosper, Robert 10

Weekly Record/American Book Publishing Record 99
Whaley, John 116
White, Herbert 51
Wilden-Hart, Marion 27
Wiley Publishing 76
Williams, Sally F. 100,125
WLN 6,7
Workstations 138-139

Yaple, Henry 110
Yankee Book Peddler 38,40,118